"We are called to be salt and light. Yet often the church fails to live differently. In our busy culture, we rarely spend time dealing with sinful areas of our lives; instead we try to sweep them under the carpet. Tim's book is a biblical and practical challenge to the very root causes of ungodly patterns of behavior. Read it and allow God to change you!"

ANDY FROST, Director, Share Jesus International

"A wonderful book for those who are serious about personal change. For so many Christians the gulf between our aspirations and the reality of our daily Christian walk is very large. Here is very helpful material to help us bridge this gap and become the whole people God intended us to be."

STEPHEN GAUKROGER, Senior Minister, Gold Hill Baptist Church

"A book about Christian growth that is neither quietistic nor moralistic is rare. A book that is truly practical is even rarer. Tim Chester's new volume falls into both categories and therefore fills a gap."

TIM KELLER, Senior Pastor, Redeemer Presbyterian Church, New York City

"There are few books that are shockingly honest, carefully theological, and gloriously hopeful all at the same time. Tim Chester's book *You Can Change* is all of these and more. He skillfully uses the deepest insights of the theology of the Word as a lens to help you understand yourself and the way of change and, in so doing, helps you to experience practically what you thought you already knew. The carefully crafted personal 'reflection' and 'change project' sections are worth the price of the book by themselves. It is wonderful to be reminded that you and I are not stuck, and it's comforting to be guided by someone who knows well the road from where we are to where we need to be."

PAUL TRIPP, President, Paul Tripp Ministries

YOU CAN CHANGE

God's Transforming Power

for Our Sinful Behavior

and Negative Emotions

TIM CHESTER

CROSSWAY

WHEATON, ILLINOIS

Library of Congress Cataloging-in-Publication Data
Chester, Tim.
    You can change : God's transforming power for our sinful
behavior and negative emotions / Tim Chester.
        p. cm.
Includes bibliographical references (p.   ).
    ISBN 978-1-4335-1231-5 (tpb)
    1. Christian life. 2. Change (Psychology)—Religious aspects—
Christianity. I. Title.
BV4599.5.C44C44   2010
248.4—dc22   2009030370

CONTENTS

INTRODUCTION

Jack started having intense struggles with lust in his teens. Twenty years or so later he's still fighting sinful fantasies. He thought marriage would sort it all out, but it didn't. He's put in place regimens of spiritual discipline, all to no avail. Alongside this has grown an addiction to pornography, an addiction strengthened by the advent of the Internet.

You'd think Carla was a respectable Christian. She doesn't swear, steal, get drunk, commit adultery, or commit any of the sins by which we measure one another's godliness. But her Christian service has little joy. Often she's irritable, often complaining.

Colin's life was turned around when he converted. He left an adulterous relationship and stopped getting drunk. But a few years later, his Christian growth seems to have plateaued. Like Carla, he looks respectable enough. But those close to him know he has a temper. He's not someone you'd ever want to cross.

If shopping were an Olympic sport, Emma would be a medal contender. She's not had an easy life, and shopping cheers her up. New clothes, something for the home, luxury foods—these are the bright spots in her life. They're her compensations. As a result money is tight, and she has little to give away to others.

Everyone said Jamal would be a great asset—godly, diligent, well-taught. But it soon became apparent that his diligence was driven by a need to prove himself. He wanted a position in the church, but his fear of failure was debilitating. There were dark moods, periods of withdrawal, tears.

Baptizing Kate had been the highlight of my year. But where to begin now? With her racism? Her drinking? Her innuendo? She'd gladly accepted the call to be ready to die for Christ, but how would she respond to the call to sobriety? How would that be good news?

Is there hope for these people? I'm convinced there is. There is the hope of change through Jesus. I know this because although I've created composite pictures and changed details, I know Jack, Carla, Colin, Emma, Jamal, and Kate.

When Jack went through an earlier version of this material with me, he stopped acting out his lust almost overnight. The sin and temptation to sin left his life. The struggle with porn has continued, with some falls, but also with many victories. Every now and then he sends me a text message asking for prayer and suggesting I "ask the question" next time we see each other.

Carla has blossomed. There hasn't been a massive change in behavior, but her attitude is radically different. She often expresses her delight in God and her amazement at his grace. She serves willingly, looks for opportunities, and takes the initiative. When she speaks of others' faults, it's with grief and love, accompanied by affirmation.

Colin has a new lease on life with a growing delight in God. He still has occasions when he feels angry. But now he knows his anger reflects a desire for control. So he responds with repentance. He's learning to trust God's sovereignty in those moments.

Emma still likes shopping. But she has other things to do now and other places to turn. She's too busy cooking for others or looking after their children. The highlights of her week are now her times with other Christians. She's learning to find refuge in God.

Jamal is a lot more relaxed. It's been a while since I've seen him in tears. It's still a challenge for him not to let failures overwhelm him, but it's been delightful to see him resting in God's grace. With this has come a freedom to serve, both at work and within the community.

It's been a joy to see Kate grow as a Christian. We've had to talk to her about some changes, while others have taken place naturally as she's seen more of Christ's glory. It's not always been straightforward, but gradually she is working it out for herself. I can't help smiling when I hear her begin, "I think maybe I ought to . . ."

Many books are written by experts. This isn't one of them. It was written out of my own struggle to change. My long battle with particular problems set me searching the Scriptures as well as writings from the past. This book shares the wonderful truths I discovered that now give me hope.

For years I wondered whether I'd ever overcome certain sins. While I can't claim to have *conquered* sin—no one ever can do so in this life—here are truths that have led to change in my life and in the lives of others. Here you will find real hope for a change.

You may be a new Christian, struggling to change the habits of your former way of life. You may be an older Christian who feels as if you've plateaued: you grew quickly when you first believed, but now your Christian life is much of a muchness. You may be a Christian who's fallen into sin in a big way, and you're wondering how you'll ever get back on track. You may be helping other Christians grow, and you can tell them how they should live, but you're not sure how to help them get there.

This book is about *hope*. It's about the hope we have in Jesus, hope for forgiveness, but also about hope for change. Not that this book will in itself change you. We're not changed by systems or rules. We need a Redeemer to set us free, and we have a great Redeemer in Jesus. This book points to Jesus and explains how faith in Jesus leads to change, what theologians call sanctification or becoming more like Jesus.

There really is hope for change. You *can* change. Maybe you've kind of given up. Like me, you may have tried many times already. Like me, you may have read books that gave you lots of things to do. Please don't despair. I believe you can experience *hope for a change*. I've read books full of good theology, and I've read books full of day-to-day advice. What this book tries to do is *connect* the truth about God with our Monday-morning struggles.

One of our problems is that we think of holiness as giving up things we enjoy out of a vague sense of obligation. But I'm convinced that holiness is *always good news*. God calls us to the good life. He's always bigger and better than anything sin offers. The key is to realize why change is good news *in your struggles with sin*.

One of our problems is that we think of holiness as giving up things we enjoy out of a vague sense of obligation. But I'm convinced that holiness is always good news.

So I want to encourage you to work on a particular concern in your life as you read the book—your "change project."

Each chapter of this book takes the form of a question that you can ask in your change project, with further questions at the end to help you explore this further. There are also reflection sections with exercises and quotes that can be used for personal meditation or group discussion. Let me urge you to read this book with a friend or group so you can provide encouragement and accountability as you work on your change projects.

You will also find additional material on the Inter-Varsity Press (England) website (www.ivpbooks.com/resources), including chapter summaries, extra reflections, and six daily Bible readings for each chapter that you can use in the days between weekly study sessions.

So let's begin with our very first question . . .

CHAPTER ONE

WHAT WOULD YOU LIKE TO CHANGE?

What would you like to change? Maybe you'd choose to change your appearance, or find a partner, or have better-behaved children. Perhaps you're seeking one more step up the career ladder, or maybe just to get onto a career ladder. Maybe you'd like to be more confident and witty, or maybe less angry or depressed, or less controlled by your emotions.

We all want to change in some way. Some of these changes are good, others not so good. But the problem with all of them is that they're not ambitious enough. God offers us something more—much, much more!

Created in God's Image

In the opening chapter of the Bible we read, "God created man in his own image, in the image of God he created him" (Genesis 1:27). We were made to be God's image on earth: to know him, to share his rule over the world, to reflect his glory. The idea is probably that of a statue of a god that represents the authority and glory of that god. But we're not to make images of the living God precisely because *we* are his image. We're God's representatives on earth. We're God's glory, displaying his likeness.

After each day of creation God declared what he had made to be "good." But on the sixth day God's verdict on a world that now included humanity was *"very* good." God's work wasn't finished until there was something in the world to reflect his glory in the world. We often excuse our actions by saying, "I'm only human." There's nothing "only" about being human: we're truly human as we reflect God's glory.

Broken Image

The problem is that this is now a broken image because humanity has rejected God. So we try to live our lives our way, and we make a mess of things. We struggle to be God's image on earth. We no longer reflect his glory as we should. God's verdict on humanity is: "All have sinned and fall short of the glory of God" (Romans 3:23). "Paul's language here," comments Sinclair Ferguson, "is loaded with the biblical motif of the divine image. In Scripture, image and glory are interrelated ideas. As the image of God, man was created to reflect, express and participate in the glory of God, in miniature, creaturely form."[1] We've failed to be the image of God we were made to be. We can't be the people we want to be, let alone the people we ought to be.

True Image

Enter Jesus, "the image of God" (2 Corinthians 4:4):

> He is the image of the invisible God, the firstborn of all creation. (Colossians 1:15)

> He is the radiance of the glory of God and the exact imprint of his nature. (Hebrews 1:3)

> And the Word became flesh and dwelt among us, and we have seen his glory, glory as of the only Son from the Father, full of grace and truth. (John 1:14)

Jesus is the glory of the Father. He makes God known in the world. He is God in human form. He shows us what it means to be the image of God and to reflect God's glory. That's why the New Testament sometimes says we should be like God and sometimes says we should be like Christ. It's because Christ is the true image of God.

Jesus shows us God's agenda for change. God isn't interested in making us religious. Think of Jesus, who was hated by religious people. God isn't interested in making us spiritual if by spiritual we mean detached. Jesus was God getting involved with us. God isn't interested in making us self-absorbed: Jesus was self-giving personified. God isn't interested in serenity: Jesus was passionate for God, angry at sin, weeping for the city. The word *holy* means "set apart" or "consecrated." For Jesus, holiness meant being set apart from, or different from, our sinful ways. It didn't mean being set apart *from* the world, but being consecrated *to* God in the world. He was God's glory *in* and *for* the world.

The glory of God is the sum of all that he is: his love, goodness, beauty, purity, judgment, splendor, power, wisdom, and majesty. The earthly life of Jesus reflected the glory of God in the goodness of his actions, the beauty of his attitudes, and the purity of his thoughts. He reflected the power of God in what appears to us a quite topsy-turvy way. He displayed the infinite freedom and grace of God not by clinging to splendor, but by voluntarily giving it up in love to rescue us (Philippians 2:6–8). Jesus is the true image of God, displaying God's glory through his life and through his death.

"At least I can put my feet up when I get home," Colin told himself as he nudged his way through the traffic. But when he walked through the door, his youngest was screaming, and his wife was going on and on about the broken vacuum cleaner. "Give me a break," he muttered, slumping into the chair.

Jamal came back to his desk with a mug of coffee. It was 11:30 P.M.—the graveyard shift. His hand wavered over the mouse. He looked at the in-tray, then clicked on the Solitaire icon. Yes, he'd work. But he'd play a quick game first.

"I'm a grown woman," Kate told herself. But she loved being in Pete's presence. He seemed to understand her so much better than her husband did. Lately her marriage had seemed hollow. She paused, then took the long way to her cubicle, past Pete's desk. She didn't want sex or even a relationship. Just a smile.

It had gone on for three years. Three years of patiently teaching and doing good, with only misunderstanding and hostility in return. He was tempted to say, "I quit—I don't need this." But instead he said, "Not my will but yours be done." A few hours later he hung on a cross, nails cutting into his limbs, lungs struggling for air, crowds spitting venom. He was tempted to say, "I quit. I'm coming down." But instead he said, "Father, forgive them." He kept going until he could cry, "It is finished."

Jesus is the perfect person, the true image of God, the glory of the Father. And God's agenda for change is for us to become like Jesus.

Jesus is the perfect person, the true image of God, the glory of the Father. And God's agenda for change is for us to become like Jesus.

And we know that in all things God works for the good of those who love him, who have been called according to his purpose. For those God foreknew he also predestined to be conformed to the likeness of his Son, that he might be the firstborn among many brothers. And those he predestined, he also called; those he called, he also justified; those he justified, he also glorified. (Romans 8:28–30)

Be imitators of God, as beloved children. And walk in love, as Christ loved us and gave himself up for us, a fragrant offering and sacrifice to God. (Ephesians 5:1–2; see also 1 Corinthians 11:1; Philippians 2:5; 1 Peter 2:21)

Whoever claims to live in [God] must walk as Jesus did. (1 John 2:6, NIV; see also 3:16–17; 4:10–11)

In Romans 8, Paul says that God uses everything that happens to us to make us like Jesus, both the good and the bad. Indeed, the bad things become in some sense good for us because they make us like Jesus. In themselves they may be evil, but God uses them for the good of those who love him, and that good is that we become more like Jesus. This isn't a letdown. We shouldn't be disappointed that the promise of good things turns out to be conformity to Christ. It's not like offering a child a meal deal from McDonald's and then giving them a McSalad. We know salad is good for us, but we'd rather enjoy a Big Mac. Jesus isn't just good for us—he is good itself. He *defines* good. The secret of gospel change is being convinced that Jesus is the good life and the fountain of all joy. Any alternative we might choose would be the letdown.

Making us like Jesus was God's plan from the beginning. God "predestined" or planned for us to be like his Son (Romans 8:29). Before God had even made the world, his plan for you and me was to make us like Jesus. And everything that happens to us is part of that plan. One day we will share God's glory and reflect that glory back to him so that he is glorified through us (v. 30).

I was dropping my daughter off at school on the day of her Easter service (she was playing Jesus, miming as the class acted out the triumphal entry). On the way we picked up Anna, a young Christian girl who'd been baptized in our church a few months earlier. As Anna was getting out of the car she shouted to my daughter, "Be a good Jesus today." "Same to you," I shouted back (though not quite quickly enough for Anna to hear).

Be a good Jesus! Our job is to study the glory of God revealed in the life and death of Jesus. We're to study his character, learn his role, and understand his motivation, so that in every situation we can improvise the part. We'll face situations that Jesus never faced. But if we understand his character well enough, we'll be able to improvise. We'll be a good Jesus.

Re-created in God's Image

I'd like to play soccer like David Beckham. I could watch videos of him in action. I could study what he does. I might even persuade him to tutor me. All this might lead to a small improvement in my abilities, but it's not going to turn me into a great soccer player.

I want to be like Jesus. I can observe him in action as I read the Gospels. I can study the life he lived and the love he showed. I could try very hard to imitate him. But at best that would lead only to a small, short-lived improvement, and indeed even that small improvement would probably only make me proud.

The great news is that Jesus is not only my example but also my Redeemer.

I need more than an example. I need help. I need someone to change me. Trying to imitate Jesus on its own only leaves me feeling like a failure. I can't be like him. I can't match up. I need sorting out. I need rescuing. I need forgiveness.

The great news is that Jesus is not only my example but also my Redeemer.

"If anyone is in Christ, he is a new creation; the old has passed away; behold, the new has come!" (2 Corinthians 5:17). When you become a Christian, something amazing happens: you are a new creation. The power of God that made the sun and stars is focused down like a laser into your heart. God steps into the world, as it were, and creates all over again. We're transformed, reborn, made new. "For God, who said, 'Let light shine out of darkness,' has shone in our hearts to give the light of the knowledge of the glory of God in the face of Jesus Christ" (2 Corinthians 4:6). At creation God spoke a word into the darkness, and there was light. He spoke a word into the chaos, and there was beauty. And now again God speaks a word through the gospel. He speaks into the darkness of our hearts, and there is light. He speaks into the chaos of our lives, and there is beauty.

What does it mean for us to be a new creation? It means we're re-created in the image of God. It means we're given new life so we can grow like Christ. And being like Christ means being like God, reflecting God's glory as God's image.

> Put on the new self, created after the likeness of God in true righteousness and holiness. (Ephesians 4:24)

> Just as we have borne the image of the man of dust, we shall also bear the image of the man of heaven [Jesus]. (1 Corinthians 15:49)

> Do not lie to one another, seeing that you have put off the old self with its practices and have put on the new self, which is being renewed in knowledge after the image of its creator. (Colossians 3:9–10)

Jesus came to remake us in God's image. He's the second Adam. Everyone takes their imprint from their father, Adam. We're made in Adam's image. That should have meant we're made in God's image, but in fact it means we're made in the broken image. We all have a built-in bias against God. But Jesus is the second Adam, and all who are united to Jesus by faith are being made new in Christ's image, the image of God as it should have been. Jesus took our brokenness, our hatred, and our curse on himself on the cross. He took the penalty of our sin and in its place gave us a new life and new love. Charles Wesley put it like this in his famous hymn "Hark! the Herald Angels Sing":

Adam's likeness, Lord, efface,
Stamp Thine image in its place:
Second Adam from above,
Reinstate us in Thy love.

"Efface" means "wipe" or "rub out." God is in the business of change. He's interested in making us like Jesus. He's restoring his image in us so that again we can know him, rule with him, and reflect his glory.

Seeing Glory and Reflecting Glory

[We are] not like Moses, who would put a veil over his face so that the Israelites might not gaze at the outcome of what was being brought to an end. But their minds were hardened. For to this day, when they read the old covenant, that same veil remains unlifted, because only through Christ is it taken away. Yes, to this day whenever Moses is read a veil lies over their hearts. But when one turns to the Lord, the veil is removed. Now the Lord is the Spirit, and where the Spirit of the Lord is, there is freedom. And we all, with unveiled face, beholding the glory of the Lord, are being transformed into the same image from one degree of glory to another. For this comes from the Lord who is the Spirit. (2 Corinthians 3:13–18)

When Moses came down from Mount Sinai after meeting with God, his face shone with the reflected glory of God, so much so that the Israelites were terrified and he had to cover his face (Exodus 34:29–35). Paul says that in a sense that veil remains. People don't recognize the glory of God because they don't recognize Christ. Their hearts shrink in fear from God's glory.

But "when one turns to the Lord, the veil is removed." When Moses was in the tabernacle before God, he could take the veil off because he was turned toward God and not toward the people (Exodus 34:34). It's the same when we turn to God in repentance. The veil that hides God's glory is taken away. Our eyes are opened to see in Christ the glory of God.

Moses coming down the mountain after meeting God was a picture of what humanity should have been. Moses radiated God's glory because he'd gazed on God's glory. That's how it should have been for all humanity.

And that's how it can be again. We can be glory-reflectors—people who radiate with divine glory. When we turn to Jesus, we see the glory of God. We see, says Paul a few verses later, "the glory of God in the face of Jesus Christ" (2 Corinthians 4:6). And when we see the glory of God, our faces shine with that glory. It transforms us so that we reflect God's glory, bringing light to the world and praise to God.

When I first studied this passage, I assumed Paul was talking about Moses' pointing to Jesus and Jesus' reflecting God's glory as God's true image. But actually Paul is saying something even more amazing: we reflect God's glory when we see God's glory in the face of Christ.

The message of this book is that change takes place in our lives as we turn to see the glory of God in Jesus. We "see" the glory of Christ as we "hear" the gospel of Christ (2 Corinthians 4:4–6). Moral effort, fear of judgment, and sets of rules can't bring lasting change. But amazing things happen when we "turn to the Lord."

The message of this book is that change takes place in our lives as we turn to see the glory of God in Jesus. We "see" the glory of Christ as we "hear" the gospel of Christ.

First, "the Lord is the Spirit, and where the Spirit of the Lord is, there is freedom." On our own, we can't be the people we want to be. We certainly can't be people who reflect God's glory. We're trapped by our emotions and desires. But when we turn to the Lord, Jesus sets us free through the Spirit. Instead of hearts shrinking in fear from God's glory, we receive hearts that delight in his glory. We're motivated no longer by the fear of law but by the opportunity to experience glory.

Second, "we all, with unveiled face, behold the glory of the Lord." When we turn to the Lord, we again begin to display God's glory. We become like Moses, our faces shining with the radiant glory of God.

Third, "we . . . are being transformed into his likeness" (NIV). When we turn to the Lord, we become more like Jesus: people of grace and truth, of love and purity.

Fourth, when we turn to the Lord, we're changed "with ever-increasing glory" (NIV). We're changed "from one degree of glory to another." We already reflect God's glory, but we reflect it all the more as we appreciate his glory in Christ. And one day we will be glorified and will enjoy him forever. The time of Moses was glorious (3:7). The present is more glorious still (3:8). The future is "ever-increasing glory" (3:18, NIV). The Puritan Thomas Watson said that sanctification, the process of change, "is heaven begun in the soul. Sanctification and glory differ only in degree: Sanctification is glory in the seed, and glory is sanctification in the flower."[2]

So whom do you want to be like? What would you like to change? Please don't settle for anything less than being like Jesus and reflecting the glory of God. And what must we do to reflect God's glory? Look on the glory of God in the face of Jesus Christ. Most of us don't live lives that are considered great by the world. For us, holiness consists not in heroic acts but in a thousand small decisions. But God gives us the opportunity to fill the mundane and the ordinary with his glory. We can be radiators of God's glory in a drab world, reflectors of his light in a dark world. Let's hear Charles Wesley again, this time from "Love Divine, All Loves Excelling":

Finish, then, Thy new creation;
Pure and spotless let us be.
Let us see Thy great salvation
Perfectly restored in Thee;
Changed from glory into glory,
Till in heaven we take our place,
Till we cast our crowns before Thee,
Lost in wonder, love, and praise.

Reflection

1. Think of specific people you consider to be Christlike. What is it about them that makes them like Jesus? What is it about them that's attractive? What's happened in their lives to make them the people they are? What do they think about themselves? What do they think about Jesus?

2. "If anyone would come after me, let him deny himself and take up his cross and follow me" (Mark 8:34). The service, submission, and suffering seen in the cross are the special marks of what it means to be like Jesus. How does the New Testament apply this to our attitude toward

- other Christians? See Romans 15:7 and Philippians 2:1–11.
- cultural influences and peer pressure? See Galatians 6:14.
- those in need? See 2 Corinthians 8:8–9 and 1 John 3:16.
- our spouse? See Ephesians 5:22–33.
- suffering? See 1 Peter 2:18–25.
- sin? See 1 Peter 4:1–2.

Change Project

What would you like to change?

Think of an area of your life that you'd like to change. It might be a type of behavior (such as lying, lust, overeating, excessive spending, or inappropriate relationships) or an emotion (for example, depression, envy, anxiety, greed, or anger). It might be a Christian virtue, a fruit of the Spirit that you feel is particularly lacking in your life.

Is your change project about changing your behavior or emotions? It's no good choosing change in someone else. You can't choose "better-behaved children" or "a better marriage." You must choose something about you, such as "shouting at my children" or "getting irritated by my spouse."

Is your change project about something specific? Try not to choose something too general, like "being a better parent." Pick a specific area of behavior or an emotion, specific enough for you to be able to remember the last time you did or felt it.

What would it mean for you to be more like Jesus?

- You may have thought about the negative behavior and emotions you would like to change. What's the positive side?

YOU CAN CHANGE

- Describe the goal of your change project.
- How would Jesus behave or think in your situation?
- Can you think of any stories or teachings of Jesus that illustrate what you should be like?

Write a summary of what you would like to change.

CHAPTER TWO

WHY WOULD YOU LIKE TO CHANGE?

Why would you like to change? Think about it for a moment. Why do you want to be more like Jesus? Why do you want to keep a lid on your temper or overcome lust or stop living in a fantasy world? Why do you want to feel less depressed or bitter or frustrated? Why do you want to be a better parent, a better husband, a better wife, a better employee? Here are three answers you may have given.

To Prove Myself to God

You may want to change so God will be impressed with you or bless you in some way or save you.

Many people think that good people go to heaven—so if you want to go to heaven, then you need to be good. We might think of heaven as a fancy nightclub with a bouncer at the door. The bouncer lets in only smartly dressed people. Anyone in jeans is turned away. So we have to smarten ourselves up to get into heaven.

Or you may think you'll be accepted on the last day because of God's grace. But you still want to impress God so he'll bless you in the meantime. "I've tried living God's way," one woman told me, "but he still hasn't given me a husband." She wanted to impress God so he'd give her what she wanted.

The instinct to self-atone runs deep in our hearts. We want to make amends for our sin on our own. But God has done it all through Christ because of his grace, his undeserved love to us. Grace is so simple to understand and yet so hard to grasp. It's not its complexity that makes it difficult. The problem is that we seem to be hard-wired to think we must do something to make God favorably disposed toward us. We want to take the credit. But all the time God is saying, "In my love I gave my Son for you. He's done everything needed to secure my blessing. I love you as you are, and I accept you in him." God can't love you more than he does now, no matter how much you change your life. And God won't love you less than he does now, no matter what a mess you make of your life. "God shows his love for us in that *while we were still sinners*, Christ died for us" (Romans 5:8).

To Prove Myself to Other People

This is often the reason I want to change: I want people to be impressed by me. We may want to fit in or win approval. We certainly don't want people finding out what we're like inside. We wear a mask to hide our real selves. Wearing the mask can be a great strain; it's like acting a role all the time. But we dare not let people see us as we really are.

One of the problems with trying to prove ourselves to other people is that they set the standard. Their standards may be ungodly, but we adopt their behavior to fit in. Or their standards may be godly, but we're living in obedience to people rather than in obedience to God. Often what happens is that we settle for living like other people even when that falls short of living like Jesus. Or we measure ourselves against other people and decide we're more righteous. We may point the finger at others' faults so we can feel better about ourselves.

Instead we should be comparing ourselves to Jesus, finding we fall a long way short of God's standards and discovering that we desperately need a Savior.

To Prove Myself to Myself

Another common reason why we want to change is so we can feel good about ourselves. When we mess up, we feel the shame of our sin. So we want to put things right. We want to think of ourselves as a "former user of porn" rather than a "porn addict." We want to say, "I used to have a problem with anger" rather than "I have a problem with anger." So when we mess up, our primary concern is that we can't think of ourselves as "a former sinner." We can't feel good about ourselves until we've put some distance between ourselves and our last "big sin." For us, sin has become first and foremost sin against ourselves. If I sin, then I've let myself down. What I feel when I sin is the offense against me and my self-esteem, not the offense against God.

Justified by Grace

What's wrong with wanting to change so we can prove ourselves to God or people or ourselves? It doesn't work. We might fool other people for a while. We might even fool ourselves. But we can never change enough to impress God. And here's the reason: trying to impress God, others, or ourselves puts *us* at the center of our change project. It makes change all about *my* looking good. It is done for *my* glory. And that's pretty much the definition of sin. Sin is living for my glory instead of God's. Sin is living life my way, for me, instead of living life God's way, for God. Often that means rejecting God as Lord and wanting to be our own lord, but it can also involve rejecting God as Savior and wanting to be our own savior. Pharisees do good works and repent of bad works. But gospel repentance includes repenting of good works done for wrong reasons. We need to repent of trying to be our own savior. Theologian John Gerstner says, "The thing that really separates us from God is not so much our sin, but our damnable good works."[1]

Deep down in all of us there is a tendency to want to prove ourselves, to base our worth on what we do. Religious people do this, but so do most non-religious people. They do a secular version in which their identity is based on performance. I feel good about myself because I'm a success at work or because I dress to impress or because I'm a great performer in bed.

As Christians, we also slip back constantly into trying to be our own savior. At the end of the Sermon on the Mount Jesus presents us with two choices, two roads, two foundations for life (Matthew 7:13–27). We might suppose the choice is between a good life and a bad life. But when you look back over the Sermon, that's not what you see. The alternative life that Jesus rejects is a good life lived for the wrong reasons. He rejects the "righteousness . . . of the scribes and Pharisees" (5:20). They think they're righteous for God, but really they're doing it for themselves (7:21–23)—"that they may be seen by others" or to manipulate God (6:1–8). Their righteousness doesn't come from the heart (5:21–48). So the options Jesus presents are self-righteousness and poverty of spirit (5:3, 20).

Another word for proving ourselves is *justify*. We want to justify ourselves—to demonstrate we're worthy of God or respectable in the eyes of other people. But we're justified only through faith in what Christ has done. When you feel the desire to prove yourself, remember you're right with God in Christ. You can't do anything to make yourself more acceptable to God than you already are. You don't need to worry whether people are impressed by you because you're already justified or vindicated by God. And what makes you feel good is not what you've done, but what Christ has done for you. Your identity isn't dependent on your change. You're a child of the heavenly King.

To some who were confident of their own righteousness and looked down on everybody else, Jesus told this parable:

> Two men went up into the temple to pray, one a Pharisee and the other a tax collector. The Pharisee, standing by himself, prayed thus: "God, I thank you that I am not like other men, extortioners, unjust, adulterers, or even like this tax collector. I fast twice a week; I give tithes of all that I get."
>
> But the tax collector, standing far off, would not even lift up his eyes to heaven, but beat his breast, saying, "God, be merciful to me, a sinner!"
>
> I tell you, this man went down to his house justified, rather than the other. For everyone who exalts himself will be humbled, but the one who humbles himself will be exalted. (Luke 18:9–14)

The Pharisee wanted to impress God. That's why he listed his achievements. Jesus said he "prayed about himself" (v. 11, NIV). And he wanted to impress other people. That's why he stood up in a prominent place (Matthew 6:5). And no doubt he was pretty impressed with himself. He certainly judged himself better than the tax collector.

The tax collector, on the other hand, didn't think he was impressive. He stood at a distance from other people. He didn't claim to be good in any way. He could only cry out to God for mercy. But, said Jesus, it was the tax collector who went home "justified." The Pharisee tried to justify himself, but he was not justified. The tax collector relied only on God's mercy, and he was justified.

I remember telling a man that his alcoholic daughter was getting baptized. He was shocked and even a little angry. He had always thought of himself as someone who was good enough for God. In fact his life was a mess in all sorts of ways, but he maintained the illusion that he was okay with God by pointing out other people's faults. At least he could think of himself as better than them. But suddenly here was his alcoholic daughter entering the kingdom of God. She wasn't good enough for God, but now that didn't seem to matter. His basis for acceptance with God was suddenly turned upside-down.

Here's the real problem with changing to impress: God has given his Son for us so that we can be justified. Jesus died on the cross, separated from his Father, bearing the full weight of God's wrath so that we can be accepted by God. When we try to prove ourselves by our good works, we're saying, in effect, that the cross wasn't enough.

Imagine you owe a huge debt that has left you languishing in poverty. Then some relatives come along and pay off your creditors. They give everything that is needed, at great cost to themselves. But then you try to give them some loose change as repayment. You let everyone know you helped repay the debt, that it was a joint effort. That would be pointless and insulting.

We don't do good works so we can be saved; we are saved so we can do good works. "For by grace you have been saved through faith . . . not a result of works. . . . For we are his workmanship, created in Christ Jesus for good works, which God prepared beforehand, that we should walk in them" (Ephesians 2:8–10). Because they can't grasp the order of salvation and good works, many unbelievers never enjoy salvation. But it's also true that because many believers don't fully grasp the order of salvation and good works, they don't enjoy the good works of holiness.

Many people change their behavior,
but their motives and desires are still wrong;
so their new behavior is no more pleasing
to God than their old behavior.

You will cleanse no sin from your life that you have not first recognized as being pardoned through the cross. This is because holiness always starts in the heart. The essence of holiness is not new behavior, activity, or disciplines. Holiness is new affections, new desires, and new motives that then lead to new behavior. If you don't see your sin as completely pardoned, then your affections, desires, and motives will be wrong. You will aim to prove yourself. Your focus will be the consequences of your sin rather than hating the sin itself and desiring God in its place.

Many people change their behavior, but their motives and desires are still wrong; so their new behavior is no more pleasing to God than their old behavior. Consider an alcoholic who gives up drink because he fears social stigma or wants to save his marriage or doesn't want to end up in the gutter. It's good that he's given up drink, but he isn't more holy in God's sight because he's still motivated by selfish desires that exclude God. Or consider a

Christian who goes to a prayer meeting to impress people or feel good about herself or avoid a Christian friend's rebuke. Her behavior has changed, but her motives and desires are unchanged. This isn't holiness (though it may be that praying with other Christians contributes to a change of affections). John Piper says, "Conversion is the creation of new desires, not just new duties; new delights, not just new deeds; new treasures, not just new tasks."[2]

The great nineteenth-century preacher Charles Spurgeon illustrates this point with the story of a humble gardener who presents a bunch of carrots to his king because he so esteems and loves his sovereign.[3] The king rewards his love with a plot of land so he can continue to bless his kingdom. A courtier sees this and thinks, "An acre of land for a bunch of carrots—what a deal!" So the next day the courtier presents the king with a magnificent horse. The wise king, discerning his heart, simply accepts the gift with a "thank you." When the courtier is disconsolate, the king explains, "The gardener gave me the carrots, but you have given *yourself* the horse. You gave not for love of me but for love of yourself in the hope of a reward." Are you feeding the hungry or are you feeding yourself? asks Spurgeon. Are you clothing the naked or are you seeking your own reward? Are you serving God or serving yourself? The Bible talks often of reward, but that reward is God himself—the joy of knowing and pleasing the God we love and in whom we delight.

We don't change so we can prove ourselves to God. We're accepted by God so we can change. God gives us a new identity, and this new identity is the motive and basis for our change.

A New Identity

Again and again in the New Testament we are called to be what we are. It's not about achieving something so we can impress. It's about living out the new identity that God gives us in Jesus.

> His divine power has granted to us all things that pertain to life and godliness, through the knowledge of him who called us to his own glory and excellence, by which he has granted to us his

precious and very great promises, so that through them you may become partakers of the divine nature, having escaped from the corruption that is in the world because of sinful desire. For this very reason, make every effort to supplement your faith with virtue, and virtue with knowledge, and knowledge with self-control, and self-control with steadfastness, and steadfastness with godliness, and godliness with brotherly affection, and brotherly affection with love. For if these qualities are yours and are increasing, they keep you from being ineffective or unfruitful in the knowledge of our Lord Jesus Christ. For whoever lacks these qualities is so nearsighted that he is blind, having forgotten that he was cleansed from his former sins. (2 Peter 1:3–9)

We don't need anything new to be godly because we already have all we need. The great and precious promises that shape our new identity enable us to be like God. Growth in godliness begins with faith in those promises. Notice the problem when someone is ineffective and unproductive. He's "forgotten that he was cleansed from his former sins." He's lost sight of his new identity.

Let's look at three ways in which the Bible talks about our new identity and see how they provide us with strong motives for change.

You Are a Child of the Father

When the right time came, God sent his Son, born of a woman, subject to the law. God sent him to buy freedom for us who were slaves to the law, so that he could adopt us as his very own children. And because we are his children, God has sent the Spirit of his Son into our hearts, prompting us to call out, "Abba, Father." Now you are no longer a slave but God's own child. And since you are his child, God has made you his heir. . . . For you have been called to live in freedom, my brothers and sisters. But don't use your freedom to satisfy your sinful nature. Instead, use your freedom to serve one another in love. (Galatians 4:4–7; 5:13, NLT; see also Romans 6:15–23)

We used to be slaves to sin. We all know this if we stop to think about it. Remember the times you've tried to change but failed. Think about how you don't live up to your own standards. Think about those New Year's resolutions that lasted only into the second week of January. We can't be the people we want to be, let alone people who are like Jesus.

But God sent his Son to buy our freedom.
We're no longer slaves with a slavemaster.
Now we're children with a Father.

We were also slaves to the law. Paul is talking about the law of Moses, but what he says is also true of any attempt to change by using a set of rules. Instead of setting us free, law crushes us. The best it can do is show us how far we are from being the people we should be. It makes us terrified of stepping out of line.

But God sent his Son to buy our freedom. We're no longer slaves with a slavemaster. Now we're children with a Father. We don't have to worry about proving ourselves because God says, "You're my child." We don't have a spirit of fear, but a Spirit who prompts us to cry, "Abba, Father." We don't have to worry about the future because God has made us his heirs so that all his resources are ours. G. C. Berkouwer says, "The adoption to sons—that is the foundation of sanctification, the only foundation. . . . In his faith each has all the possession he requires and can therefore freely and lovingly devote his entire life to the service of his fellowman."[4]

We were slaves of sin, and now we are children of God. It would be crazy to go on living as slaves and not as children. Freedom doesn't mean we can sin; that's not freedom, that's going back into slavery. Imagine an alcoholic whose addiction has wrecked his life. Someone kindly puts him through rehab, and after several months he leaves, free from his addiction. He's not going to say, "I'm free at last, so I'm going to get drunk." That's not freedom. That's returning to his old slavery.

It was Sophie's first day with her adoptive parents. She stalked nervously around her new home, fearing one of the beatings she was used to getting if something got broken. The toys in her room went untouched; she couldn't quite believe they were hers. At dinner she secretly stuffed food into her pocket: you never knew where your next meal would come from when you were on the streets. That night she felt so alone in her big room. She would have cried if she hadn't long since learned to suppress her emotions.

Now listen to her new mother one year later: "She crawled into bed with me last night because she was having a bad dream. She curled up next to me, put her head on my chest, told me that she loved me, smiled, and went to sleep. I nearly cried with contentment."

Sophie had a new identity on day one. She'd become a child in a new family. But initially she still lived like a child of the street. Her actions and attitudes were shaped by her old identity. Christians too have a new identity. And we're to live out our new identity, to be what we are. So don't live like a slave when you can live like a child of the King of heaven.

You Are the Bride of the Son

> Husbands, love your wives, as Christ loved the church and gave himself up for her, that he might sanctify her, having cleansed her by the washing of water with the word, so that he might present the church to himself in splendor, without spot or wrinkle or any such thing, that she might be holy and without blemish. (Ephesians 5:25–27)

The church is the bride of Christ. He has loved us, wooed us, cleansed us, rescued us, and won us. Our relationship with Christ is a relationship of love and intimacy. It is a union—an exclusive union.

Why do I bring my wife a cup of tea in bed in the mornings? It's not because I need to make her mine. She's already my wife, just as Christ is already my bridegroom. It's not because I need to make sure she won't leave me. She's committed herself to me with the covenant promises of marriage, just as Christ has committed himself to me with covenant promises. It's not even so she'll treat me well. She often treats me well even when I treat her badly, just as Christ is always gracious toward me even when I don't deserve it. No, I try to please my wife because I love her and because she loves me. I delight in delighting her. So it is with Christ. Christ is our lover, our partner, and our bridegroom, and so we live for him, want to please him, and do what he asks. The more my wife loves me, the more I find myself loving her. Christ has loved me with infinite love, giving himself for me on the cross. He loved me when I was unlovely. If I'm holy, clean, or radiant, it's only because he made me so. And so I love him and live for him.

The Bible often describes sin as "adultery" (Jeremiah 3:7–8; 5:7; Ezekiel 23:37; Matthew 12:39; James 4:4; Revelation 2:22). Sin is like adultery because it's a betrayal of our true and best love. Why would you commit that sin? The "love" of an adulterous lover is no love at all. Sin doesn't love us. It tries to use us, abuse us, enslave us, control us, and ultimately destroy us. Sin takes from us and gives nothing in return. It may use enticing and seductive lies. It may promise the world. But it's all lies. Sin never brings true and lasting satisfaction. Why would you leave a husband as good, loving, gracious, strong, able, and beautiful as Jesus for some cheap alternative? This is how Paul put it to the Christians in Corinth: "For I feel a divine jealousy for you, since I betrothed you to one husband, to present you as a pure virgin to Christ. But I am afraid that as the serpent deceived Eve by his cunning, your thoughts will be led astray from a sincere and pure devotion to Christ" (2 Corinthians 11:2–3). One woman put it to me like this: "As a child I dreamed of my wedding day, of walking down the aisle in a beautiful white dress. In none of my dreams was my dress covered in dirt and grime."

We're to live out our new identity, to be what we are. And this means being a pure, devoted, loving bride of Christ.

You Are the Home of the Holy Spirit

> Flee from sexual immorality. Every other sin a person commits is outside the body, but the sexually immoral person sins against his own body. Or do you not know that your body is a temple of the Holy Spirit within you, whom you have from God? You are not your own, for you were bought with a price. So glorify God in your body. (1 Corinthians 6:18–20)

The temple in the Old Testament was a holy place. Nothing impure was allowed. Now we are the holy place of God. Our lives, and our life together as a Christian community, are sacred spaces, consecrated to God.

Christians have come to use the term *sanctification* to describe the lifetime process of change into Christ's likeness. But when the New Testament talks about Christians being sanctified, it usually refers to a past, definitive action by God.[5] We have been consecrated by God for his service and made new by the Holy Spirit. Our role is to live out this new identity as God's holy ones or saints. (*Transformation* might be a better term for what we call sanctification, but *sanctification* is now the term commonly used for this process of transformation.)

Imagine you've done the cleaning at home because you have guests coming. You've scrubbed the floors, cleaned the windows, tidied the rooms, and dusted the furniture. Everything is spick-and-span. And then you pop out to get some flowers from the shops, through the rain and mud. What do you do when you get back? Do you tramp your muddy feet through the house and shake out your wet clothes? No; you carefully take everything off at the door. You want to keep your home clean for your guests. The Holy Spirit has cleansed and washed us. He's given us a new start and a new life. He's come to make his home in us. He's consecrated our lives as his temple. Why would you want to mess that up by bringing in your dirty habits or returning to your filthy sins? Would you want a friend to live in a trash bin?

We're to live out our new identity, to be what we are. And that means being a holy temple for God's Spirit.

The challenge for us is to let these new identities define us on Monday mornings. It's easy to sing about being a child of God or the bride of Christ on a Sunday. The challenge is to think of ourselves as children of God in the classroom on a Monday morning when our classmates jeer at the way we live. The challenge is to think of ourselves as the bride of Christ in the office when the banter is coarse and the ambitions are worldly and as the home of the Holy Spirit in the supermarket, when everything feels mundane and dreary.

Freedom and Love

Let's sum up our motive for change: *to enjoy the freedom from sin and delight in God that God gives to us through Jesus.* I want to highlight four things arising from this definition.

All too often we think of holiness as giving up the pleasures of sin for some worthy but drab life. But holiness means recognizing that the pleasures of sin are empty and temporary, while God is inviting us to magnificent, true, full, and rich pleasures that last forever.

First, *growing in holiness is not sad, dutiful drudgery.* It's about joy. It's discovering true joy—the joy of knowing and serving God. There is self-denial, sometimes hard and painful, but true self-denial leads to gaining your life (Mark 8:34–37). There will be times when we act out of duty, but we do this believing that duty leads to joy, that denying ourselves leads to gaining our life (Mark 8:35–36).[6] How often have you reluctantly dragged yourself out on a cold night to pray with others only to find yourself energized and blessed?

Second, *change is about living in freedom*. We refuse to go back to the chains and filth of our sin. We live in the wonderful freedom that God has given us. We're free to be the people we should be.

Third, *change is about discovering the delight of knowing and serving God*. Our job is to stop wallowing around in the dirt and instead to enjoy knowing God, to give up our cheap imitations and enjoy the real thing. All too often we think of holiness as giving up the pleasures of sin for some worthy but drab life. But holiness means recognizing that the pleasures of sin are empty and temporary, while God is inviting us to magnificent, true, full, and rich pleasures that last forever.

Fourth, *becoming like Jesus is something that God gives to us*. It's not an achievement that we offer to him. It's enjoying the new identity he has given us in Christ. It begins with his work for us. He has set us free from sin and offers us a relationship with himself.

It's as if there are two feasts: the feast of God and the feast of sin. We're invited to both. God invites us to find satisfaction in him. Sin entices us, with its lies, to look for satisfaction in sin. So we're double-booked. All the time we have to choose which feast to attend. This is God's invitation to us:

> Come, everyone who thirsts,
> come to the waters;
> and he who has no money,
> come, buy and eat!
> Come, buy wine and milk
> without money and without price.
> Why do your spend your money for that which is not bread,
> and your labor for that which does not satisfy?
> Listen diligently to me, and eat what is good,
> and delight yourselves in rich food. (Isaiah 55:1–2)

Sin promises so much. But it doesn't deliver, and it charges a high price—broken lives, broken relationships, broken hopes. Ultimately the wages of sin is death. But God offers us a feast that satisfies. He offers delight for our souls. The motivation for change and holiness is this: God's feast is so much better! And the price tag reads, "No cost." There's no charge. It's his gift to us.

Which feast are you going to attend today?

Reflection

1. Take a look at the following paragraphs. I've taken some verses from the Bible and made them say the *opposite* of what they actually say. See if you can turn them back into what they really say. You can check by looking at Romans 5:1–2 and Ephesians 2:8–10.

- When we prove ourselves by living a good life, we have peace with God through what we do. It's what we do that gives us access to God's blessing and a good standing in people's eyes. This means we can worry less about whether we'll share God's glory.
- It's by changing that our problems will be sorted out, through working hard. It's up to us. This is what we can do for God. We're saved by what we do, so we can prove ourselves. If we do the good works that God plans for us, then we can become God's masterpiece, new people in Christ Jesus.

2. Identify when sin made one of the following promises in your experience. *What did it actually deliver?*

- Sin promises fun and excitement, but it delivers pain and tragedy.
- Sin promises freedom, but it delivers slavery and addiction.
- Sin promises life and fulfillment, but it delivers emptiness, frustration, and death.
- Sin promises gain, but it delivers loss.
- Sin promises that we can get away with it, but the fact is, we don't.[7]

Change Project

Why would you like to change?

Do you really want to change?

- Does the thought of becoming like Jesus make you feel sad?
- Do you think your life will become boring, unsatisfying, and hard?

- Do you think of giving up sin as an unpleasant duty you need to do to win God's approval?

Do you want to change for the wrong reasons?
Do you sometimes think:

- God won't bless me today because I've let him down?
- God will answer my prayers today because I've been good?
- I need to make it up to God because I've sinned?
- I need to change so God will accept me on the final day?

If you answered yes to any of these questions, you may be trying to change to impress God.

Do you sometimes:

- make sure people know about the good things you're doing?
- tell "little white lies" to cover up your failings?
- imagine people being impressed because you're so spiritual?
- feel like you've let yourself down when you sin?

If you answered yes to any of these questions, you may be trying to change to impress people or to feel good about yourself.

What do you think will happen if you're successful in your change project?
What difference will it make to:

- God's love for you?
- people's opinion of you?
- how you view yourself?

What can you do to strengthen your desire to change?
If you suspect you don't really want to change, think what you could do to strengthen your resolve. If you suspect you may want to change for the wrong reasons (to impress God, to impress people, or to feel good about yourself), then think what you could do to focus on your new identity in Christ.

Here are some ideas:

- Compare slavery to sin with being a child of God. Compare the sin of adultery to being the bride of Christ. Compare the filth of sin with being a clean home for the Holy Spirit.
- Memorize Romans 5:1–2, Ephesians 2:8–10, or Titus 3:5–8. Use these verses to speak to your heart when you think in wrong ways.
- On the cross Jesus cried out, "It is finished." Imagine yourself answering back, "Not quite. I need to finish the job. I still need to win God's blessing." Think how ridiculous and insulting to God this is.
- Imagine two homes side by side. In one, God is hosting his feast. In the other, sin is hosting its feast. Compare the two feasts. What satisfaction do they offer? How lasting and real is that satisfaction? What price must you pay?

Write a summary of why you would like to change, putting it in a way that resonates for you. Add some ideas on how you could strengthen your desire to change.

CHAPTER THREE

HOW ARE YOU GOING TO CHANGE?

"Please forgive me and set me free." I don't know how many times I've prayed this prayer; it must be in the hundreds. "Father, here I am again, confessing the same sin to you again." Every time I have to remind myself of God's merciful character and gospel promises. I am forgiven. But I also really want to change.

Have you despaired of ever changing? Do you think you're a lost cause? Maybe you think it's different for you. Other people can change, but your history or temptations or problems make it different for you.

The glorious good news of Jesus is that you and I can change.

Part of the problem is we often try to change in the wrong way.

Trying to Change Ourselves

Frustrated by my lust, I wrote out a vow. This was it. Never again. I noted the date and imagined looking back in months to come with satisfaction that my struggle was history. But it didn't last long. It didn't work. It *couldn't* work, as I'd have realized if I'd paid attention to Colossians 2:20–23:

> If with Christ you died to the elemental spirits of the world, why, as if you were still alive in the world, do you submit to regulations—"Do not handle, Do not taste, Do not touch" (referring to things that all perish as they are used)—according to human precepts and teachings? These have indeed an appearance of

wisdom in promoting self-made religion and asceticism and sever-
ity to the body, but they are of no value in stopping the indulgence
of the flesh.

Maybe you think making vows or undertaking other disciplines is very spiritual. I certainly thought so at the time. But Paul
says it's only the "appearance of wisdom." In reality they have
"no value in stopping the indulgence of the flesh." Wasn't that the
truth? Sadly, I had to learn that lesson the hard way. The Puritan
John Flavel said, "We are more able to stop the sun in its course
or make rivers run uphill as by our own skill and power to rule
and order our hearts."[1]

It seems our first instinct when we want to change is to do
something. We think activity will change us. We want a list of do's
and don'ts. In Jesus' day, people thought they could be pure through
ceremonial washing. Today it can be spiritual disciplines or sets of
laws. I've tried these approaches. I've written out little rituals to
perform every morning. I've tried to regulate my behavior with lists.
Many of these things are good in themselves, and we'll discover the
role they can play in helping us grow in holiness. But our rituals and
disciplines can't change us.

---

*External activities can't change us, says Jesus,
because sin comes from within, from our hearts.
Our rituals might change our behavior
for a while, but they can't change our hearts.*

"Then are you also without understanding?" [Jesus] asked. "Do
you not see that whatever goes into a person from outside cannot
defile him. . . . What comes out of a person is what defiles him. For
from within, out of the heart of man, come evil thoughts, sexual
immorality, theft, murder, adultery, coveting, wickedness, deceit,

sensuality, envy, slander, pride, foolishness. All these evil things come from within, and they defile a person." (Mark 7:18–23)

External activities can't change us, says Jesus, because sin comes from within, from our hearts. Our rituals might change our behavior for a while, but they can't change our hearts. And so they can't bring true and lasting holiness. We need heart change.[2]

What Law Can and Can't Do

In the early church, many people advocated living by the law of Moses. We become Christians by faith, they said, but we keep going by following the law. At first sight, that looks like a good option. After all, this list is God-given. It produces people who appear to be very serious about their faith. But Paul would have none of it. We continue as we began, he said—namely, through faith in what Jesus has done for us.

> Therefore, as you received Christ Jesus the Lord, so walk in him, rooted and built up in him and established in the faith, just as you were taught, abounding in thanksgiving. (Colossians 2:6–7)

> You foolish Galatians! Who has bewitched you? Before your very eyes Jesus Christ was clearly portrayed as crucified. I would like to learn just one thing from you: Did you receive the Spirit by observing the law, or by believing what you heard? Are you so foolish? After beginning with the Spirit, are you now trying to attain your goal by human effort? (Galatians 3:1–3, NIV)

Our Christian lives began when we received the Spirit by believing in Christ crucified, not when we finally managed to observe the law. It's foolish to think we can now take over and finish the job through human effort. Imagine being carried across the Niagara Falls by a skilled tightrope walker. Halfway across you have a choice. You can let him carry you the rest of the way, or you can tell him you think it would be better if you walked the rest of the way under your own steam. *We become Christians by faith in Jesus, we stay Christians by faith in Jesus, and we grow as Christians by faith in Jesus.* J. C. Ryle wrote, "If we would be sanctified, our course is clear and plain—*we must begin with Christ.* We must go to Him as sinners, with no plea but that of utter need, and cast our souls on Him by faith. . . . If we would grow in holiness and become more sanctified, we must *continually go on as we began,* and be ever making fresh applications to Christ."[3] It's not just that trying to live by laws and disciplines is useless—it's a backwards step. It's a step back into slavery, which ends up undermining grace and hope (Galatians 4:8–11; 5:1–5).

What the law *does* do is show us we can't change ourselves or make ourselves good enough for God. The purpose of the law is to point to the righteousness that Jesus offers (Romans 3:21–22). The law isn't meant to be the starting point for change. It's meant to bring us to an end of ourselves and so drive us into the arms of Jesus.

Repenting of Righteousness

We all have a strong tendency to want to live by a list of rules—it's called legalism. I was talking to a group of students about lifestyle issues. They kept asking specific questions: What car can I buy? What should I do with my savings? How much should I spend on clothes? They wanted a list or a law. But even if we could create such a list for every occasion, it wouldn't work.

Legalism is appealing for two reasons. First, it makes holiness manageable. A heart wholly devoted to God is a tough demand, but a list of ten rules I can cope with. That was the motivation of the expert in the law who asked Jesus, "Who is my neighbor?" He wanted to justify himself, to tick the "love for neighbor" box. But Jesus' story of the good Samaritan blew his manageable system apart. Second, legalism makes holiness an achievement on our part. "Yes, I was saved by grace," the legalist says, "but I'm the godly person I am today because I've kept this code of behavior or practiced these spiritual disciplines." One of its by-products is comparison with other people. We check whether we're holier than other people or look down on those who don't appear to be as good as we are.

No one thinks of himself as a legalist. Such persons just think of themselves as someone who takes holiness seriously. After all, it has the *"appearance of wisdom"* (Colossians 2:20–23). But if you want to see a legalist, take a look in the mirror. Deep in the heart of all of us is the proud desire to prove ourselves. Sin is wanting to live our lives our own way without God. The terrible irony is that we even want to overcome sin our own way without God. The struggle against legalism was not done and stored away two thousand years ago in Galatia or five hundred years ago at the Reformation. The battle with legalism takes place every day in our hearts.

This means we need to repent not only of our sin but also of our "righteousness" when we think of it as *our* righteousness, which we do to prove ourselves and which we think makes us better than other people.

> If anyone else thinks he has reason for confidence in the flesh, I have more: circumcised on the eighth day, of the people of Israel, of the tribe of Benjamin, a Hebrew of Hebrews; as to the law, a Pharisee; as to zeal, a persecutor of the church; as to righteousness under the law, blameless. But whatever gain I had, I counted as loss for the sake of Christ. Indeed, I count everything as loss because of the surpassing worth of knowing Christ Jesus my Lord. For his sake I have suffered the loss of all things and count them as rubbish, in order that I may gain Christ and be found in him, not having a righteousness of my own that comes from the law, but that which comes through faith in Christ, the righteousness from God that depends on faith. (Philippians 3:4–9)

Paul's claims to righteousness were impressive. He had more reason than most to have confidence in his achievements. When it came to keeping lists, he was *"blameless."* But when he saw Christ, he realized that all his assets were actually liabilities. Everything he had previously considered to be on the profit side of his balance sheet actually had to be counted as loss. He discovered that rules-based righteousness is not really righteousness at all. He had to repent of *"a righteousness of my own that comes from the law"* so that in its place he could receive *"the righteousness from God that depends on faith."*

The songwriter Bob Kauflin describes a three-year period of hopelessness in his life characterized by depression, panic attacks, and itching. He confessed this hopelessness to a pastor who, to his great surprise, said, "I don't think you're hopeless enough." Kauflin thought he was joking, but the pastor explained, "If you were completely hopeless, you'd stop trusting in what you think you can do to change the situation and start trusting in what Jesus Christ has already done for you at the cross." "A light went on," says Kauflin. For months afterward, every time he felt anxious or hopeless, he would say to himself, "I am a hopeless person, but Jesus Christ died for hopeless people."[4]

Change Is God's Work

It is God himself who sanctifies us (1 Thessalonians 5:23). Other therapies can modify behavior. Drugs can suppress the more extreme symptoms of some problems. But only God can bring true and lasting change. And that's because only God can change our hearts.

John the Baptist said, "I have baptized you with water, but he will baptize you with the Holy Spirit" (Mark 1:8). He was talking about Jesus. John knew he could only make people outwardly clean. But Jesus changes us on the inside through the Holy Spirit. He transforms, cleanses, and changes hearts. John was proclaiming the fulfillment of an Old Testament promise:

> I will sprinkle clean water on you, and you shall be clean from all your uncleannesses, and from all your idols I will cleanse you. And I will give you a new heart, and a new spirit I will put within you. And I will remove the heart of stone from your flesh and give you a heart of flesh. And I will put my Spirit within you, and cause you to walk in my statutes and be careful to obey my rules. (Ezekiel 36:25–27)

Jesus does what legalism can never do: he gives us a new heart and a new spirit. Without this inner transformation, we can never please God. People aren't changed by therapy or analysis—not even biblical analysis. They are changed by God. God is in the business of change.

The Liberating Work of the Father

> Our fathers disciplined us for a little while as they thought best; but God disciplines us for our good, that we may share in his holiness. No discipline seems pleasant at the time, but painful. Later on, however, it produces a harvest of righteousness and peace for those who have been trained by it. (Hebrews 12:10–11, NIV)

God the Father is intimately involved in our lives, and the purpose of that involvement is that we might "share in his holiness." Human fathers do their best to instill in their children good values and behavior. The divine Father is engaged in the same process, but his discipline is perfect. He always "disciplines us for our good." The Father is using all the circumstances of our lives to make us more holy. His work in our lives will ultimately produce "a harvest of righteousness and peace."

This doesn't mean that bad things in our lives are a direct retribution for some specific misconduct. God never punishes us since Christ has already paid the price of our sin in full. God always and only disciplines us to strengthen our relationship with him. It is always an act of love. It's a sign that we are truly God's children (Hebrews 12:8). God uses hardship (12:7) to weaken our allegiance to this world and set our hope on the world to come, to weaken our dependence on worldly things and strengthen our faith in him (Romans 5:1–5; James 1:2–4; 1 Peter 1:6–9). Even the sinless Son of God was made perfect by God through suffering (Hebrews 2:10).

I was recently pruning the apple tree in my garden. Apple tree branches send shoots out in every direction. This means that shoots criss-cross, getting in each other's way and making the tree less fruitful. For two hours I clambered about in the tree, creating a big pile of branches, which will end up on the fire. As I was working, I couldn't help thinking of Jesus' words, "I am the true vine, and my

Father is the vinedresser. Every branch in me that does not bear fruit he takes away, and every branch that does bear fruit he prunes, that it may bear more fruit" (John 15:1–2). Just as I was cutting off every shoot that was heading in the wrong direction, so God cuts out every desire that is heading away from him. I'm hoping the result of my pruning will be a big crop of apples. God's pruning always makes us more fruitful.

Trainees in a new workplace may be given a range of tasks and experiences to equip them. They learn partly through teaching, partly on the job. They're exposed to difficult circumstances so they gain confidence and experience. God the Father has designed a complex and full training package for each believer. Every circumstance of our lives is part of this lifelong development program. He uses "all things" for our good, and that good is that we become like his Son (Romans 8:28–29). Day by day he is working out his plan until we "share in his holiness."

The Liberating Work of the Son

What shall we say then? Are we to continue in sin that grace may abound? By no means! How can we who died to sin still live in it? Do you not know that all of us who have been baptized into Christ Jesus were baptized into his death? We were buried therefore with him by baptism into death, in order that, just as Christ was raised from the dead by the glory of the Father, we too might walk in newness of life. For if we have been united with him in a death like his, we shall certainly be united with him in a resurrection like his. We know that our old self was crucified with him in order that the body of sin might be brought to nothing, so that we would no longer be enslaved to sin. For one who has died has been set free from sin. (Romans 6:1–7)

A death and resurrection have taken place in us. My old sin-oriented self has died. I've been given a new life with new desires. The "old self" is the person we used to be, the person we were in Adam (Romans 5:12–21). This old self was under the power of sin. We were slaves to sin. But now we've been united to Christ—a reality symbolized in baptism. We've been united with Christ in his death: his death becomes the death of our old self. And we've been united with Christ in his resurrection: we've been given a new self or a new life. Jesus sets us free from the penalty of sin, i.e., death. But Jesus also sets us free from the power of sin, i.e., slavery. We're free to live for God. Telling a slave to be free is to add insult to injury. But telling a *liberated* slave to be free is an *invitation* to enjoy his new freedom and privileges.

We continue to struggle with sin. We're like a freed slave who still jumps at his old master's voice. We're like a man with a healed leg who still limps out of habit. We're like a former prisoner who still wakes at prison hours. That's why Paul must urge us, "Let not sin . . . reign in your mortal body, to make you obey its passions" (Romans 6:12). But something decisive has happened. It's no longer inevitable that we'll sin when we face temptation. We have the power to say no to temptation.

We also have a new motivation to battle with sin: we're no longer under law, but under grace. This is counterintuitive. People think that law and legalism will best motivate us to strive to do what's right. But it's grace that enables us to live for God. "For sin will have no dominion over you, since you are not under law but under grace" (Romans 6:14). Grace wins our hearts. Sinclair Ferguson says, "Only when we turn away from looking at our sin to look at the face of God, to find his pardoning grace, do we begin to repent. Only by seeing that there is grace and forgiveness with him would we ever dare to repent and thus return to the fellowship and presence of the Father. . . . Only when grace appears on the horizon offering forgiveness will the sunshine of the love of God melt our hearts and draw us back to him."[5] William Romaine, one of the leaders of the Great Awakening, says:

> No sin can be crucified either in heart or life unless it first be pardoned in conscience, because there will be want of faith to receive the strength of Jesus, by whom alone it can be crucified. If it be not mortified in its guilt, it cannot be subdued in its power.[6]

We're changed when we look at Jesus, delight in Jesus, commune with Jesus. But no one can embrace Jesus if still guilty of sin. And no one will embrace Jesus if still feeling the guilt of sin. So change begins only when we come under grace with its message of divine pardon and welcome. Only then will we "with confidence draw near to the throne of grace, that we may receive mercy and find grace to help in time of need" (Hebrews 4:16).

This how my friend Matt describes his experience at one Christian school:

> All teenagers hate rules, but this school had the most ridiculous rules. Boys had to part their hair from right to left because parting it from left to right was rebellious! They even had pictures in the school handbook with "Christian boy" and "rebellious boy" written under the specified hair styles. Part your hair wrongly and you got detention. And detention involved copying out entire chapters of the Bible. Trousers could not have outside seams or patch pockets. Wear the wrong trousers and you had an hour copying Psalm 119. And it gets worse. In class you weren't allowed to make eye contact with other students because that was considered communication and, yep, you got Psalm 119 in detention. No chewing gum, no eating candy, no sitting with girls. Boys and girls had separate stairways and walkways. Break any of these and the Psalmist would be waiting for you. These rules drove me mad. I tried to break as many as I could. In the eight months I was there I had 32 detentions. They were supposed to mould my character and they did that all right: into the most rebellious kid possible! They made me angry, bitter, rebellious and rude—though I did know the Psalms well in the end.

Matt is now a bouncer, and he looks like one. He is big, broad, has his head shaved, and doesn't have a neck. Rule upon rule didn't change him. Instead they sent him off the rails. But you'd never guess it now as the children sit on his lap in church and he exudes a passion to tell others about Jesus. What turned his life around was the grace of Christ. What a set of rules could never do, grace did.

When Jesus talks about the Father as a gardener, he talks about himself as the vine. What gives life to branches is their connection to the vine. It's that connection that makes them fruitful. What makes us fruitful is our connection to Jesus. "Remain in me," Jesus says, "and I will remain in you. No branch can bear fruit by itself; it must remain in the vine. Neither can you bear fruit unless you remain in me" (John 15:4, NIV). If you saw a branch without grapes, you'd conclude it was dead. And if you saw someone who didn't bear the fruit of holiness, you'd have good reason to suppose he or she wasn't a true Christian. But it's not bearing fruit that makes us a Christian, any more than grapes make a vine alive. It's the other way around. The vine gives life to a branch, and grapes are a sign that the branch has life from the vine. In the same way, Christ produces good works in us, and our good works are a sign that we have life in him.

The Liberating Work of the Spirit

Transformation is the special work of the Holy Spirit. God chose us "to be saved, through sanctification by the Spirit and belief in the truth" (2 Thessalonians 2:13). We have been chosen "according to the foreknowledge of God the Father, in the sanctification of the Spirit, for obedience to Jesus Christ and for sprinkling with his blood" (1 Peter 1:2). There was a time when labels on electronic toys often said, "Batteries not included." You opened your long-awaited Christmas present only to find you couldn't make it work. The gospel is a gift that comes with "batteries included." God gives us power through the Holy Spirit to make our new life work. John Berridge put it like this:

> Run, John, and work, the law commands,
> Yet finds me neither feet nor hands;
> But sweeter news the gospel brings,
> It bids me fly and lends me wings.[7]

Our sanctification begins with the Spirit's work of regeneration or rebirth (John 3:3–8). The Spirit gives us new life. It's the Spirit's life in us that enables us to trust in Jesus as our Savior (faith) and submit to Jesus as our Lord (repentance). And it's the Spirit's life in us that enables us to grow in our faith and obedience. The great Puritan John Owen puts it like this: "Regeneration is the putting into the soul of a new, real spiritual law of life, light, holiness and righteousness, which leads to the destruction of all that hates God. . . . Regeneration produces an inward miraculous change of heart. . . . Our minds now have a new, saving supernatural light to enable them to think and act spiritually."[8]

> I say, walk by the Spirit, and you will not gratify the desires of the flesh. For the desires of the flesh are against the Spirit, and the desires of the Spirit are against the flesh, for these are opposed to each other, to keep you from doing the things you want to do. (Galatians 5:16–17; see 5:13–25; Romans 8:1–17)

The Spirit gives us the desire to do what is right and opposes our old sinful desires to do what is wrong. Our job is to follow the Spirit. Imagine a child being taught to paint by her father.[9] Her father wraps his hand around hers, guiding each stroke of the brush. The Spirit is God's guiding hand in our lives. Whenever we want to do the wrong thing or react in the wrong way, the Spirit opposes those wrong desires. And we should be led by the Spirit. Whenever we want to do the right thing, that is the Spirit at work. We should be led by the Spirit even though the sinful nature doesn't like it. When you feel this conflict, go with the Spirit. Walk in step with the Spirit. Follow those Spirit-prompted desires.

We should be led by the Spirit even though the sinful nature doesn't like it. When you feel this conflict, go with the Spirit.

It's as simple as that. Often I get nervous as I entrust young Christians to the Spirit's promptings. I'm not sure it's good enough. I want to give them some rules or wall them in. But that's legalism.

That's why Paul reminds us that "if you are led by the Spirit, you are not under the law" (Galatians 5:18). Some ethical issues are complicated, but most of the time it's clear what's wrong ("sexual immorality, impurity," and so on) and what's right ("love, joy, peace, patience, kindness, goodness, faithfulness, gentleness, self-control") (vv. 19–23). Love is the summary of it all (v. 14). The Christian life is not as complicated as we sometimes make it. Only two commands matter: to love God and to love others (Mark 12:28–31; Romans 13:8–10). Everything else is there simply to flesh out what this love involves. The Spirit gives us a desire to love and opposes our selfish desires.

The law was to be on people's hearts (Deuteronomy 6:6). But in reality it's sin that's engraved on our hearts (Jeremiah 17:1). So God promised to write his law on our hearts through the Spirit (Jeremiah 31:31–34; Romans 7:6). The Spirit is our "rule." We are like a bride who cooks lovely meals, not because she is bound by some rulebook but because of the love she has for her husband.[10] It's the Spirit who gives us this new desire for Christ our husband and who guides us toward what pleases him through God's Word. "God is working in you, giving you the desire and the power to do what pleases him" (Philippians 2:13, NLT).

- The Father is intimately involved in our lives so that our circumstances train us in godliness.
- The Son has set us free from both the penalty and the power of sin so that we now live under the reign of grace.
- The Spirit gives us a new attitude toward sin and a new power to change.

The combined forces of the Trinity are at work in our lives to set us free and make us holy.

Change Is in Our DNA

"No one born of God makes a practice of sinning, for God's seed abides in him, and he cannot keep on sinning because he has been born of God" (1 John 3:9). At first sight this verse can leave us worrying whether we're truly Christians. "No one who is born of God will continue to sin," says John (vv. 6–10, NIV). But I continue to sin (as John himself reminds me in 1:8), so maybe I'm not born of God? But take a closer a look and this passage offers tremendous hope. John writes to give us confidence (5:13).

It's true that we sin and break the law, but Jesus "appeared to take away sins" (3:4–5). It's true that anyone who sins belongs to the devil, but Jesus "appeared . . . to destroy the works of the devil" (vv. 7–8). Without Jesus we can never break free from sin's grip. But Jesus came to set us free from sin and destroy Satan's power. He's begun a process in us that will end with our becoming like God: "we are God's children now . . . we know that when he appears we shall be like him, because we shall see him as he is" (v. 2). That process isn't yet complete, so we still fall into sin. But we're no longer enslaved by sin. We can change.

More than that, John says holiness has now been written into our DNA! "No one born of God makes a practice of sinning, for God's seed abides in him, and he cannot keep on sinning because he has been born of God" (v. 9). That's the negative: not sinning is in our DNA. Later John states the positive: "Beloved, let us love one another, for love is from God, and whoever loves has been born of God and knows God" (4:7). Love is in our DNA.

As I grow older, I look more like my father. It's not that I'm making a special effort to look like him. It's in my genes. It's the same, says John, with our heavenly Father. John didn't know about DNA, so he uses the word "seed," but it's the same idea. When we were born, we received a nature with a built-in tendency toward sin. When we were born of God, we received a new nature with a built-in tendency toward holiness.

I can't make myself look like my father. I could attempt not to look like him. I could grow my hair long and dye it green. It's the same with sanctification. I sometimes go out of my way to look unlike my heavenly Father. It's a bit pathetic—like dyeing my hair green—and I always end up looking worse. But change is in my DNA. John says the end of the change process is certain: I will be like Jesus when I see him as he is (3:2). That means change is not only possible, it's inevitable!

I used to think sanctification was a bit like pushing a boulder up a hill. It was hard, slow work, and if you lost concentration you might find yourself back at the bottom. But it's more like a boulder rolling down a hill. There's something inevitable about it, because it's God's work, and God always succeeds. The sad thing is that often I try to push the boulder back up the hill. I say in effect, "Don't change me yet—I like doing that sin."

Sanctified by Faith

Sometimes people say conversion is all God's work, but sanctification is a cooperation between us and God. Neither statement is entirely true. Conversion is all God's work, but we have a responsibility to respond with faith and repentance. But it turns out that faith and repentance are also God's work in us, his gift to us. God opens blind eyes. God grants repentance (Mark 8:18–30; 2 Corinthians 4:4–6; 2 Timothy 2:25). That's why conversion is entirely an act of God's grace. But, at God's initiative and with God's help, we're involved. And it's the same with sanctification. Sanctification is God's work. But we're not passive. We have to respond with faith and repentance. And again it turns out that faith and repentance are God's work in us. So salvation from start to finish is God's work, in which we are active participants through faith and repentance by the grace of God. We work hard, but then say with Paul, "It was not I, but the grace of God that is with me" (1 Corinthians 15:10). "Work out your own salvation with fear and trembling, for it is God who works in you, both to will and to work for his good pleasure" (Philippians 2:12–13).

There are important differences between justification (being right with God) and sanctification (becoming like God). When I'm first converted, Christ's righteousness is credited to me (Romans 4:4–8). I'm united with Christ, so that his vindication is my justification

(Romans 4:25). This is what gives me confident hope for the day of judgment (Romans 5:1–2, 9–10). God counts me right with him solely because of what Christ has done outside of me without any change on my part. Sanctification, however, takes place within me. It's all about me changing. Justification is a change of my status in God's sight; sanctification is a change of my heart and character.[11]

> *Justification is a change of my status in God's sight; sanctification is a change of my heart and character.*

But we shouldn't separate justification and sanctification. They're joined together so that sanctification follows where justification leads. Underlying both is our union with Christ by faith. We are justified because we're united to Christ, the Righteous One. But union with Christ also brings with it a change of life. John Calvin says:

> By faith we grasp Christ's righteousness, by which alone we are reconciled to God. Yet you could not grasp this without at the same time grasping sanctification also. . . . Therefore Christ justifies no one whom he does not at the same time sanctify. These benefits are joined together by an everlasting and indissoluble bond.[12]

What justification and sanctification have in common is that they take place through faith in Christ. "The Bible teaches that we are sanctified *by faith*."[13] By faith we find God more desirable than anything sin offers. By faith we continue to be united to Christ, the source of our new life. By faith we embrace the new identity that is ours by grace. By faith we follow the new desires of the Spirit. Sometimes the Reformed and evangelical traditions treat sanctification as a human achievement made in response to the divine act of justification. We're justified by faith in Christ's work, but, it's supposed, we're sanctified by our own efforts or even by law-keeping. An emphasis on sanctification by faith is, I believe, more faithful both to the Reformed tradition and to the Bible.[14] We begin the Christian life through faith and repentance, and we continue the Christian life through faith and repentance. John Owen says, "Holiness is nothing but the implanting, writing and realizing of the gospel in our souls."[15] When the crowd asks Jesus what God expects of them, he replies, "This is the only work God wants from you: Believe in the one he has sent" (John 6:28–29, NLT).

It means we need a kind of re-conversion each day. The first of Martin Luther's famous Ninety-five Theses was this: "When our Lord and Master Jesus Christ said, 'Repent,' he willed that the whole life of believers should be one of repentance."[16] Each day we turn afresh in faith and repentance toward God. We rediscover our first love all over again so that we're not tempted to engage in spiritual adultery. "The key to continual and deeper spiritual renewal and revival is the *continual re-discovery of the gospel*."[17]

In Greek mythology, the Sirens would sing enchanting songs, drawing sailors irresistibly toward the rocks and certain shipwreck. Odysseus filled his crew's ears with wax and had them tie him to the mast. This is like the approach of legalism. We bind ourselves up with laws and disciplines in a vain attempt to resist temptation. Orpheus, on the other hand, played such beautiful music on his harp that his sailors ignored the seductions of the Sirens' song. This is the way of faith. The grace of the gospel sings a far more glorious song than the enticements of sin, if only we have the faith to hear its music.

Reflection

1. Think of all the things you bring to your relationship with Christ. Divide them into a profit column (valuable contributions to the relationship) and a loss column (worthless contributions to the relationship).

Read Philippians 3:4–9 and review what should be in the profit and loss columns. The only thing in the profit account is "the righteousness from God that depends on faith" (v. 9).

2. "For our sake he made him to be sin who knew no sin, so that in him we might become the righteousness of God" (2 Corinthians 5:21). This verse speaks of our new status before God (justification). But that status is the basis for change in our lives (sanctification). Personalize this by inserting a sin with which you struggle. For example, "God made Christ who had no lust to be punished as a *porn addict* for me, so that in Christ I might become *sexually pure* before God."

God made Christ who had no _____[insert your sin] to be _____[insert what your sin makes you] for me, so that in Christ I might become _____[insert the opposite of your sin] before God.

Change Project

How are you going to change?

How have you tried to change in the past?

- What have you done to try to change in the past?
- What has worked?
- What hasn't worked?

Are you trying to change yourself?

- Have you ever made vows or created lists to help you change?
- Do you ever compare yourself with other people?
- Do you need to repent of your own efforts to change?

How is God at work in your life?

- How have you changed over the past two years?
- How did that change come about?
- Can you see God at work in your life? Can you see signs of the liberating work of the Father, Son, and Spirit?

How are you responding to God's work of change?

- God is changing his children into the family likeness. Are there ways in which you are trying *not* to look like God?
- Do you feel that you have reached a plateau in your Christian life, as if your Christian growth has leveled off? Why do you think this is?
- Are there sins with which you've struggled for many years? Do you believe you can change?

Write a summary of how you are going to change. Write down the aspect of God's work of change that especially gives you confidence that you can change.

CHAPTER FOUR

WHEN DO YOU STRUGGLE?

When do you sin? In what kind of situations do you act in a wrong way or experience negative feelings? What makes you depressed, angry, bitter, irritated, or frustrated? When are you prone to temptation? Think about your change project. Think of the last time you remember doing or feeling it. What was going on? What set you off? What wound you up? What made you depressed, angry, or frustrated? Is there a pattern?

Life is tough. All of us face challenging situations. Yours may be difficult family relationships or sickness or financial worries. It may be people who rile you up or a dead-end job. It may be singleness or a loveless marriage. Peer pressure may push you toward sin, or it may be the stress of having too much to do. We are messed-up people living in a messed-up world.

God Cares about Our Struggles

"I have surely seen . . . [I] have heard . . . I know their sufferings . . . I have come down." That was God's message to his suffering people in Egypt (Exodus 3:7–8). Our heavenly Father sees our struggles. He hears our cry for help. He's concerned about what we're going through. We often think no one knows or no one cares. But God knows, and God cares. We're allowed to struggle. It's legitimate to feel pain, disappointment, and heartache. Many of the Psalms talk about struggle, and by talking about it, they give it a home in God's Word. God the Father sees our struggles.

But God doesn't just look on our struggles from a distance. He rolled up his sleeves, came down, got involved, and experienced our struggles firsthand. Ultimately God entered our world when the Son of God became human. Jesus knows what it is to be hungry, assaulted, rejected, tired, lonely, tempted, needy, opposed, and busy. He faced poverty, injustice, temptation, and betrayal. More than all that, on the cross he was forsaken by his Father (Mark 15:34). Jesus shared our struggles. Jesus wasn't a special being floating above all the mess. We mustn't settle for a Sunday-school picture of Jesus dressed in a sparkling white robe surrounded by happy children. He was a real person, living in a world of dirt, pain, and frustration.

God doesn't just look on our struggles from a distance. He rolled up his sleeves, came down, got involved, and experienced our struggles firsthand.

"I'm not talking to them about it," we sometimes say. "They won't understand. Nobody knows what it's like to be me." But God does know what it's like.

Jesus fully shared our humanity, and "because he himself has suffered when tempted, he is able to help those who are being tempted." He "sympathize[s] with our weaknesses," and so we can "with confidence draw near to the throne of grace, that we may receive mercy and find grace to help in time of need" (Hebrews 2:14–18; 4:14–16).

Not only has God experienced our struggles, he is with us through the Spirit here and now. God says, "Fear not, for I have redeemed you; I have called you by name, you are mine. When you pass through the waters, I will be with you; and through the rivers, they shall not overwhelm you; when you walk through fire you shall not be burned, and the flame shall not consume you" (Isaiah 43:1–2).

On the night before he died, Jesus said to his disciples, "I will ask the Father, and he will give you another Helper, to be with you forever, even the Spirit of truth" (John 14:16–17). People often tell me they need a counselor. Often another Christian can help us understand what's going on in our hearts. But we have a great Counselor already: we have the Spirit of Truth. And Jesus says he is with us forever. The word Jesus uses to describe the Spirit has the ideas of advocate, counselor, and comforter all rolled up into one word. Jesus goes on to say:

> The Helper, the Holy Spirit, whom the Father will send in my name, he will teach you all things and bring to your remembrance all that I have said to you. Peace I leave with you; my peace I give to you. Not as the world gives do I give to you. Let not your hearts be troubled, neither let them be afraid. (John 14:26–27)

Jesus gives us peace by giving us the Holy Spirit as our Counselor to point us to God's gracious promises. Jesus isn't being naive, nor is he promising an easy ride. Later he says, "In the world you will have tribulation" (John 16:33). We will have troubled circumstances. But we don't need to have troubled hearts because we have a divine Comforter who reminds us of the truth.

God Does Something about Our Struggles

I sat opposite her, her face puffy and red after many hours of crying. The man she had hoped to marry had just died in an accident. There was faith, but also questioning and great grief. I count it a great privilege to be with people in the crisis moments of their lives. We go many layers beyond the superficial to the deep things of the heart. But being with her was pretty much all I could offer. I couldn't bring him back, nor heal the wound in her heart. Having someone with us is a great comfort in the valley of the shadow of death. But God does so much more than just put an arm around our shoulders.

First, he uses our struggles. "We know that for those who love God all things work together for good . . . to be conformed to the image of his Son" (Romans 8:28–29). It's easy to believe that about the good things that happen to us. It's not easy to believe it about the bad things. But the Bible is clear that God uses suffering to make us like Jesus. Evil is evil. It's painful, confusing, and real. Behind it is the malevolent mind of Satan. But God uses it for his bigger purposes (see Genesis 50:20; Acts 4:27–28). For all eternity your past experience of evil will enhance your eternal experience of glory. You'll be shaped by it in beautiful ways.

> We rejoice in our sufferings, knowing that suffering produces endurance, and endurance produces character, and character produces hope, and hope does not put us to shame, because God's love has been poured into our hearts through the Holy Spirit who has been given to us. (Romans 5:3–5)

> Count it all joy, my brothers, when you meet trials of various kinds, for you know that the testing of your faith produces steadfastness. And let steadfastness have its full effect, that you may be perfect and complete, lacking in nothing. (James 1:2–4)

> In this [hope] you rejoice, though now for a little while, if necessary, you have been grieved by various trials, so that the tested genuineness of your faith—more precious than gold that perishes though it is tested by fire—may be found to result in praise and glory and honor at the revelation of Jesus Christ. (1 Peter 1:6–7)

What's striking about these passages is the way they all begin with a call to rejoice. We can rejoice in suffering when we make the connection between suffering and growth. Sometimes we see it in our lives; sometimes we can only hold on to it by faith. But we rejoice because we trust that God is using all things for our good—the good of becoming like Jesus.

Second, God not only uses our struggles, he promises to bring them to an end. He has taken our sufferings on himself to end our sufferings. On the cross Jesus took God's wrath on himself in our place, freeing us from God's curse. He promises a new world without sin or pain. His resurrection is the beginning of a new creation, which will come to completion at the end of history—a new creation in which God himself will "wipe away every tear" and in which "death shall be no more, neither shall there be mourning, nor crying, nor pain anymore" (Revelation 21:3–4). "In this you rejoice, though now for a little while, if necessary, you have been grieved by various trials" (1 Peter 1:6).

Our Struggles Reveal Our Hearts

Why do we do the things we do? Why do we get angry, frustrated, irritable, or depressed or, for that matter, happy, excited, or content? Why do we lie, steal, fight, and gossip? Why do we dream, fantasize, envy, and plot? Why do we overwork and overeat? Why do our children misbehave? Why do adults have sex outside marriage? Why are we worried about what people think? Why do we fail to be the parents, spouses, or employees we should be? Why do we speak when we shouldn't and keep quiet when we should speak? Where do evil thoughts, sexual immorality, theft, murder, adultery, greed, and malice all come from? Jesus gives us the answer: "For from within, out of the heart of man, come evil thoughts, sexual immorality, theft, murder, adultery, coveting, wickedness, deceit, sensuality, envy, slander, pride, foolishness. All these evil things come from within, and they defile a person" (Mark 7:21–23).

My Behavior Comes from My Heart

Where does sin come from? From within. Out of men's hearts. From inside. According to the Bible, *the source of all human behavior and emotions is the heart.* "Heart" in the Bible means more than the organ that pumps blood around the body. It refers to the inner person or the essential self. "As in water face reflects face, so the heart of man reflects the man" (Proverbs 27:19). *Heart* is shorthand for our thinking and desires. The root cause of my behavior is *always* my heart. What we see is behavior and emotions, and it's easy to focus on changing behavior and emotions. But lasting change is achieved only by tackling their source—the heart. Jesus says:

> No good tree bears bad fruit, nor again does a bad tree bear good fruit, for each tree is known by its own fruit. For figs are not gathered from thornbushes, nor are grapes picked from a bramble bush. The good person out of the good treasure of his heart produces good, and the evil person out of his evil treasure produces evil, for out of the abundance of the heart his mouth speaks. (Luke 6:43–45)

If you see a bush with thorns, you know it's not a fig tree. It has the DNA of a thornbush, and it's this DNA that causes it to grow thorns rather than figs. It's the same with people. Our sinful behavior reflects the sin in our hearts. Every sinful action and negative emotion reveals a problem in our hearts.

Our struggles and temptations often trigger sin, but they never cause it. The root cause is always the heart and its sinful desires.

When I left home at age nineteen, my father gave me a verse: "Keep your heart with all vigilance, for from it flow the springs of life" (Proverbs 4:23). Sadly, it took me twenty years to realize what an important verse it was. The *New Living Translation* paraphrases it thus: "Guard your heart above all else, for it determines the course of your life." All our actions flow from the heart.

My Circumstances Trigger My Heart

Only when we understand the role of our hearts can we truly understand the role of our circumstances in sin. Our struggles and temptations often trigger sin, but they never cause it. The root cause is always the heart and its sinful desires. We choose how we respond to circumstances, and what determines our choices are the thinking and desires of our hearts.

People don't see it like this. Think of the last time you were angry. Not all anger is bad. God himself is angry about sin. Good anger is an emotional response to the right things (sin and injustice) in the right way (controlled and desiring good). But think about the last time you were angry in a destructive way. What made you angry? We normally point to external factors: "They didn't treat me with respect." "Someone smashed my car." "They never see it my way." But James says that what causes fights and quarrels are the desires that battle within (James 4:1–2). Anger arises because our desires are thwarted or threatened. External pressures have an impact on our behavior *via our hearts*. We can't blame our circumstances.

> Let no one say when he is tempted, "I am being tempted by God," for God cannot be tempted with evil, and he himself tempts no one. But each person is tempted when he is lured and enticed by his own desire. Then desire when it has conceived gives birth to sin, and sin when it is fully grown brings forth death. (James 1:13–15)

James is talking to Christians facing "trials of various kinds" (v. 2). If we persevere, God will reward us with "the crown of life" (v. 12). What we can't do is blame God. It's not God's fault if I fail to persevere. I can't say, "It was my upbringing, my biology, my personal history, or my circumstances." James tells us that what causes a person to be enticed by temptation is "his own desire." Selfish desires lead to sin, says James, and sin leads to death. The deadly effects of sin in our lives, emotions, and relationships stem from the evil desires of our hearts. Jerry Bridges warns against using the language of defeat to describe sin. That suggests being overwhelmed by external factors and can therefore suggest that we are not to blame. The language of disobedience more accurately describes what's happening.[1]

Our background can shape our sinful response. Some people express anger through foot-stomping and shouting; others opt for silence and withdrawal. Whether you fly into a rage or apply the silent treatment may depend on your upbringing, on what you've learned from the people around you. But both rage and silence are anger, and the root cause of that anger lies in our hearts.

If you saw me in my study at 7:30 in the morning reading my Bible or praying, you might think me the most godly of men. There I am, calm, peaceful, trusting. But observe me half an hour later as I attempt to marshal my daughters out of the door for school and you'd see a man who's far from godly. I used to think of myself as that calm, gentle person—the 7:30 me—and concluded I was pretty godly! If I'm provoked to sin, then the problem must be whatever provoked me. But I've come to realize that the real me is the person who is revealed when the sinful desires of my heart are exposed by trying circumstances and annoying people. The real me is revealed when I'm too tired to keep up the pretense.

We Sin Because We Do Not Trust God and Do Not Worship God

Our struggles reveal our hearts. But that means they're a great opportunity to tackle the root causes of our sinful behavior and negative emotions.

Sin happens when we believe lies about God instead of God's word and when we worship idols instead of worshipping God.

So what is going on in our hearts? The Bible says two things are always happening in our hearts. Hebrews 4:12 speaks of "the thoughts and intentions of the heart."

- We think, interpret, believe, trust.
- We desire, worship, want, treasure.

Human beings are always interpreters and always worshippers. We're interpreters who form explanations for what's happening to us. And we were made by God to worship him; so worship is hard-wired into our being.

There is a twofold problem in the heart: what we think or trust and what we desire or worship. Sin happens when we don't trust God above everything (when we interpret in the wrong way) and when we don't desire God above everything (when we worship the wrong thing). Sin happens when we believe lies about God instead of God's Word and when we worship idols instead of worshipping God. Listen to Ed Welch:

> In our hearts we are always actively worshipping, trusting, desiring, following, loving, or serving something or somebody. When Scripture speaks of the heart, it typically is emphasizing that we live before God, in all things and at all times. We respond to him either by trusting in him or trusting in our self-serving idols.
>
> These spiritual allegiances of the heart are sometimes hidden, but like the quality of fruit on a tree, the heart will eventually reveal itself in word and deed (Luke 6:43–45). Any violation of God's law is an expression of the heart, as is faith and obedience. Our emotions are also, more often than not, animated by the orientation of our hearts. When our worship is true, we experience joy, peace, love, and hope, even in difficult situations. When our worship is false, and the things we desire are unattainable or impotent, we can be grieved, bitter, depressed, angry, or fearful. Our emotions usually mean something, and it is wise to ask, "What are my emotions saying?" "What are they pointing to?"[2]

Destructive or sinful behavior such as lying, manipulation, violence, theft, adultery, addictions and eating disorders, and negative or sinful emotions such as anxiety, depression, envy, guilt, bitterness, and pride all arise when our hearts don't trust God as we should and don't worship God as we should. So the answer is faith and repentance. We need to

- trust God instead of believing lies = faith.
- worship God instead of worshipping idols = repentance.

The key is to make the link between our specific sins and the lies and idols in our hearts. This is what we'll explore in the following chapters.

Reflection

How would you complete the following statements?

- When I get angry it's usually because . . .
- When I get down it's usually because . . .
- When I disobey God it's usually because . . .

Think about your answers. Do they describe what triggers your behavior or the root cause of your behavior? Do they describe what is going on in your heart?

Change Project

When do you struggle?

What are your struggles?

- What pressures do you regularly face?
- Who are the people you find it difficult to cope with?
- What situations cause you to worry or get angry or brood or overreact or dream of revenge or justify yourself or become despondent?
- What did you think or believe in those moments?
- What did you want or worship in those moments?

When do you struggle with the problem you've chosen in your change project?

- When do you often do it or feel it?
- What triggers it?
- Are there any patterns?
- What do you think or believe in those moments?
- What do you want or worship in those moments?

What's going on in your heart?

- What did you want, desire, or wish for?
- What did you fear? What were you worrying about?
- What did you think you needed?
- What were your strategies and intentions designed to accomplish?
- In what or in whom were you trusting?
- Whom were you trying to please? Whose opinion of you counted?
- What were you loving? What were you hating?
- What would have brought you the greatest happiness, pleasure, or delight? What would have brought you the greatest pain and misery?[3]

Write a summary of when you sin and what is going on in your heart.

We'll be thinking more about what's going on in our hearts in the next chapters.

CHAPTER FIVE

WHAT TRUTHS DO YOU NEED TO TURN TO?

Lee suffered from panic attacks. In time they became self-reinforcing. The fear of an attack would induce another one. He would phone me three or four times a week. Each time I would speak the truth to him. We developed some catchphrases: "God is greater than your thoughts." "Not what if? but what is, and what is, is that God is in control." The truth set him free. The truth of God's sovereignty brought peace, and with it a new realization of the centrality of God and his glory. It wasn't instantaneous. Each day brought a fresh struggle to believe. Another of our catchphrases was, "Yesterday was a victory, today is another battle." But in time the panic attacks went away.

We find true freedom in embracing God's reign over our lives and trusting his reign to be wise and good. This is the interpretation of life that brings joy and peace. But in the Garden of Eden the serpent persuaded Eve to doubt the goodness of God's rule. Satan offered a different worldview, one that portrayed God as a tyrant whose rule should be rejected. Eve took the fruit because she believed this lie about God. Sin began with humanity disbelieving God's word.

Behind Every Sin and Negative Emotion Is a Lie

Sinful acts always have their origin in some form of unbelief. *Behind every sin is a lie.* The root of all our behavior and emotions is the heart—what it trusts and what it treasures. People are given over to sinful desires because "they exchanged the truth about God for a lie" (Romans 1:24–25).

> Now this I say and testify in the Lord, that you must no longer walk as the Gentiles do, in the futility of their minds. They are darkened in their understanding, alienated from the life of God because of the ignorance that is in them, due to their hardness of heart. They have become callous and have given themselves up to sensuality, greedy to practice every kind of impurity. (Ephesians 4:17–19)

Humanity's problem is futile thinking, darkened understanding, and ignorant hearts. This is the cause of indulgence, impurity, and lust. We sin because we believe the lie that we are better off without God, that his rule is oppressive, that we will be free without him, that sin offers more than God.

This is true of every sin and every negative emotion.

We sin because we believe the lie that we are better off without God, that his rule is oppressive, that we will be free without him, that sin offers more than God.

Often we can identify specific lies behind specific sinful acts and emotions. I may envy, steal, or be anxious about money because I believe the lie that consumer goods give meaning to my life or because I believe that God doesn't care about me. I may commit adultery or get depressed about my singleness because I believe the lie that intimacy with another person will give me more than God can give me.

Not many people think of themselves as someone who believes lies. But every time we don't trust God's word we're believing something else, and that something is always a lie. If I get angry when

I'm struck in traffic, it's because I don't trust God. I believe the lie that God isn't in control or that his purposes for me are not good. If I overwork it's because I don't trust God, perhaps because I believe the lie that I need to prove or justify myself. This is a radical view of sin. It means many of our negative emotions are sinful because they're symptoms of unbelief—the greatest sin and the root sin. Whenever we're depressed or bitter, it's because we believe God isn't being good to us or that he's not in control. "Whatever does not proceed from faith is sin" (Romans 14:23).

Not many Christians think of themselves as unbelievers. After all, we normally use the term to describe people who aren't Christians at all. Most of us can happily endorse the creeds of our church. But our problems rarely arise from a lack of belief in a confessional or theoretical sense, though this may be the case. More often they arise from functional or practical disbelief. The problems lie in the gap between what we believe in theory and what we believe in practice.

On Sunday morning I sing of my belief in justification by faith (confessional faith), but on Monday morning I still feel the need to prove myself (functional disbelief). Or I may believe I'll be acquitted on the day of judgment, but I still want to justify myself in an argument tomorrow. I may affirm that God is sovereign (confessional faith), but I still get anxious when I can't control my life (functional disbelief). Sanctification is the progressive narrowing of the gap between confessional faith and functional faith.

The Truth Shall Set You Free

Recognizing that behind every sin is a lie not only gives us a radical view of sin, it points us to the road out of sinful behavior and emotions. That road is trust in God.

> The path of the righteous is like the light of dawn, which shines brighter and brighter until full day. The way of the wicked is like deep darkness; they do not know over what they stumble. My son, be attentive to my words; incline your ear to my sayings. Let them not escape from your sight; keep them within your heart. For they

are life to those who find them, and healing to all their flesh. Keep your heart with all vigilance, for from it flow the springs of life. (Proverbs 4:18–23)

Proverbs describes the road of trust in God as "like the light of dawn." Maybe you feel as if you're in darkness, trapped in your behavior, with negative emotions weighing heavily upon you. Seeing them as symptoms of unbelief can be like the first gleam of dawn. Hopes dawns with the realization that the answer is found in looking to God. It's a long road that takes a lifetime to travel, but with every step the light of God's goodness shines "brighter and brighter until full day." We follow this road by paying attention to the Word of God (vv. 20–21). God's Word is our road map. The gracious promises of God give true life and health (v. 22). The truth will guard our hearts and therefore our lives (v. 23).

> Thus says the LORD: "Cursed is the man who trusts in man and makes flesh his strength, whose heart turns away from the LORD. He is like a shrub in the desert, and shall not see any good come. He shall dwell in the parched places of the wilderness, in an uninhabited salt land. Blessed is the man who trusts in the LORD, whose trust is the LORD. He is like a tree planted by water, that sends out its roots by the stream, and does not fear when heat comes, for its leaves remain green, and is not anxious in the year of drought, for it does not cease to bear fruit." (Jeremiah 17:5–8)

Jeremiah uses a different picture. People who trust in their own strength are like barren trees in a desert. Maybe that's how you feel, as if you are running on empty, thirsty for something more. Life feels fruitless and pointless. God says that people who trust in him are like trees planted by water that never fail to bear fruit. That doesn't mean they have an easy life. The scorching heat comes on them. But their roots go down into the refreshing waters of God's Word. Faith in God sustains them and keeps them fruitful in the midst of adversity.

"Everyone who commits sin is a slave to sin," says Jesus (John 8:34). People feel trapped in their negative behavior or emotions.

They feel they can't change. And in one sense they can't. Trying to change behavior alone doesn't work because the lies that create that behavior are still there. But Jesus says, "If you hold to my teaching, you are really my disciples. Then you will know the truth, and the truth will set you free" (John 8:31–32, NIV). Just as lies about God lead to the slavery of sin, so the truth about God leads to the freedom of service (Galatians 5:1, 13). The truth that sets us free is the gospel ("if you hold to my teaching"). Freedom is found in the truth that we were made to worship God, to serve God, to trust God. Freedom is found in acknowledging that we are responsible for the mess we have made of our lives, that our problems are rooted in our hearts, that we deserve God's judgment, that we desperately need God. Freedom is found in accepting that God is in control of our lives, that he is gracious, that he forgives those who come to him in faith. Paul says, "For the grace of God that brings salvation has appeared to all men. It teaches us to say 'No' to ungodliness and worldly passions, and to live self-controlled, upright and godly lives" (Titus 2:11–12, NIV).

Often we can be specific about the truth that will set us free from the lies that enslave us. If I'm enslaved by my worries, then freedom is found in trusting the sovereign care of my heavenly Father. If I'm enslaved by the need to prove myself, then freedom is found in trusting that I'm fully justified in God's sight through the atoning work of Christ.

Seeing, Knowing, Embracing, Desiring

Change takes place as we see the glory of God in Jesus, as we know the truth that sets us free. But seeing and knowing don't properly capture the force of understanding we need. When this chapter asks what truths you need to turn to, it doesn't mean simply acquiring information or agreeing with statements. It's possible to see without seeing (Jeremiah 5:21; Ezekiel 12:2; Matthew 13:13). Nineteenth-century theologian Charles Hodge says that true knowledge of Christ "is not the apprehension of what he is, simply by the intellect, but also . . . involves . . . the corresponding feeling of adoration, delight, desire and [contentment]."[1] Seeing and knowing Christ isn't just receiving information but means recognizing him as the one who is altogether lovely. It's embracing the truth about God and delighting in it.

Psalm 19:10 says the truth of God's Word is "sweeter also than honey." Suppose you've never tasted honey. You know it's sweet because you've heard of its sweetness from reliable sources. But that's a very different kind of knowledge from the knowledge of honey's sweetness you get when you take a big bite and fall in love with its taste.[2] We need to "taste and see that the LORD is good" (Psalm 34:8). Paul prays that "the eyes of [our] hearts may be enlightened in order that [we] may know the hope to which he has called [us], the riches of his glorious inheritance in the saints" (Ephesians 1:17–18, NIV). Our prayer should be that we will not only comprehend truth with the eyes of our mind but will embrace truth with "the eyes of [our] hearts." This is the key to change. The Puritan Walter Marshall says, "The more good and beneficial we apprehend God to us to all eternity, doubtless the more lovely God will be to us, and our affections will be the more inflamed towards him."[3] Seeing God—delighting in God—desiring God—desiring God more than we desire sin.

Preaching to Our Hearts

We need to become preachers. We need to learn to preach to our own hearts. The psalmist says, "Bless the LORD, O my soul, and forget not all his benefits" (Psalm 103:2). To whom is he speaking? The answer is to himself. The famous preacher Martyn Lloyd-Jones said, "Have you realized that most of your unhappiness in life is due to the fact that you are listening to yourself instead of talking to yourself?"[4] We need to take every thought captive (2 Corinthians 10:3–5). Our problem, says Sinclair Ferguson, is that "we think with our feelings."[5] We don't always *feel* joy in God, but by faith we can tell ourselves that he *is* our joy. When we find ourselves tempted to engage in sinful behavior, or when we find that our emotions are getting the better of us, we need to speak truth to our hearts. Say the truth to yourself repeatedly so that it sinks in: "God is all I need." Say it slowly: "God . . . is . . . all . . . I . . . need." Say it out loud. Say it back to him: "You are all I need." C. S. Lewis says, "The moment you wake up each morning, all your wishes and hopes for the day rush at you like wild animals. And the first job of each morning consists in shoving them all back; in listening to that other voice, taking that other point of view, letting that other, larger, stronger, quieter life come flowing in."[6]

It helps if you can identify the specific lies behind your sin and the corresponding truths that will set you free. But you don't have to be able to analyze your heart in detail. It's the truth of the gospel that brings change. This is how John Newton describes the liberating power of Jesus' name:

> How sweet the name of Jesus sounds
> In a believer's ear!
> It soothes his sorrows, heals his wounds,
> And drives away his fear.
>
> It makes the wounded spirit whole,
> And calms the troubled breast;
> 'Tis manna to the hungry soul,
> And gives the weary rest.
>
> Dear name! The rock on which we build;
> Our shield and hiding-place;
> Our never-failing treasury, filled
> With boundless stores of grace.

I want to identify four life-changing truths about God. Psalm 62:11–12 says, "Once God has spoken; twice have I heard this: that power belongs to God, and that to you, O LORD, belongs steadfast love." The key truths that God declares about himself are his *greatness and glory* ("power belongs to God") and his *goodness and grace* ("to you, O LORD, belongs steadfast love").

1. God is great—so we do not have to be in control.
2. God is glorious—so we do not have to fear others.
3. God is good—so we do not have to look elsewhere.
4. God is gracious—so we do not have to prove ourselves.

There's much more to be said about God than is covered by these four truths, but they offer a powerful diagnostic tool for addressing most of the sins and emotions with which we struggle.[7]

1. God Is Great—So We Do Not Have to Be in Control

Traveling at the speed of light (186,000 miles a second), you would encircle the earth seven times in one second and pass the moon in two seconds. At this speed it would take you 4.3 years to reach our nearest star and 100,000 years to cross our galaxy. There are thought to be at least 100,000,000,000 galaxies in the universe. It would take 2,000,000 light-years to reach the next closest galaxy and 20,000,000 to reach the next cluster of galaxies. And you have still only just begun to explore the universe.

All this was created when our God simply spoke a word. In fact, Isaiah tells us that he marked off the heavens with the breadth of his hand (Isaiah 40:12). It's a spatial metaphor for a God who exists outside space, but it gives us a sense of the scale of God: the whole universe fits into his hand. Hold your hand up: the universe is that big to God! Hebrews 1:3 says Jesus sustains it all by the power of his word. He "works all things according to the counsel of his will" (Ephesians 1:11). In a mysterious way that involves human freedom, God orders every event and determines every action: "The king's heart is a stream of water in the hand of the LORD; he turns it wherever he wills" (Proverbs 21:1). Even evil actions are part of his plan. The conspiracy that sent Jesus to the cross was the result of evil choices by human beings. Yet "they did what [God's] power and will had decided beforehand should happen" (Acts 4:28, NIV). From the movement of atoms to the complexities of human history, God sustains and rules all.

I wonder if you've ever lost work on a computer because it crashed. It happened to me the other day. I let out a loud "Nnoooo!" as my head hit my desk. To whom was I speaking? The reality is, though I might not have admitted it, I was crying out a "no" to God and his sovereignty. I was rejecting his sovereign rule over my life. "No, God, you don't know best. Your rule is not good. Otherwise why would you let this happen?"

Alan is sitting on the train. Inexplicably it's stopped just outside the station. He's getting angry because it looks as if he'll miss his hospital appointment.

Beth is stressed. Replacing the family car has wiped out their savings. Now she's worried that they won't have enough money at the end of the month. When her husband comes home with an expensive-looking bunch of flowers to cheer her up, she just bursts into tears.

Colin's getting very frustrated. He's trying to get a new community project going, but everything seems to be going wrong. As a result, he's getting irritable with his children.

Dorothy's lying awake at night thinking about her friend Eileen. Eileen seems to be slipping into postnatal depression. Dorothy's looked after Eileen's baby a couple of times, but she has her own responsibilities. She wishes she could do more.

In Mark 4:35–5:43 Jesus displays his control over the natural world, over the spirit world, over sickness, and even over death. The stories are told to highlight Jesus' complete authority. He brings a girl back from death as easily as you or I might rouse someone from sleep. All the time Mark presents the alternatives of fear and faith. The disciples are afraid in the storm. Among them are experienced fishermen, so this is no irrational phobia. Yet Jesus rebukes them: "Why are you so afraid? Have you still no faith?" (4:40). The people see the demon-possessed man in his right mind and fear the power that tamed him (5:15). The sick woman comes before Jesus with "fear and trembling" (5:33). But Jesus speaks a word of peace to her. Because of her faith, she has no need to fear God. Jesus' word to Jairus is the punch line of the section: "Do not fear, only believe" (5:36). God is greater than all the things we fear. These stories don't teach that we'll never face sickness or death. Instead they teach us that we needn't fear the circumstances of life because God is in control. He works good for us in every circumstance. He'll bring us safely home to glory. Death is not the last word: the last word is "Talitha cumi!"—"Little girl, I say to you, arise" (5:41).

What happens when you don't truly trust God's sovereign control? You might try to take control yourself in harmful ways, through manipulation or domination. You might wear yourself out with busyness or frustration. You might make your security and wealth a bigger priority than God's kingdom (Luke 12:22–31). Or you might worry (Philippians 4:6–7). We become preoccupied with the bills, and money becomes our main obsession. All because we don't believe our Father knows what we need. Jesus goes straight to the heart of the problem—our little faith:

> Which of you by being anxious can add a single hour to his span of life? . . . O you of little faith! And do not seek what you are to eat and what you are to drink, nor be worried. For all the nations of the world seek after these things, and your Father knows that you need them. Instead, seek his kingdom, and these things will be added to you. (Luke 12:25–31)

We often associate the sovereignty of God with theological debates. But for all of us it's a daily practical choice.

We often associate the sovereignty of God with theological debates. But for all of us it's a daily practical choice. For me, the issue is escapism. I have to choose between a fantasy in which I'm sovereign and the real world in which God is sovereign, between my false sovereignty and God's real sovereignty. When I feel like running away, I have to choose to find refuge in God.

2. God Is Glorious—So We Do Not Have to Fear Others

One common reason why we sin is that we crave the approval of people or we fear their rejection. We "need" the acceptance of others, and so we're controlled by them. The Bible's term for this is "fear of man." "The fear of man lays a snare, but whoever trusts in the LORD is safe" (Proverbs 29:25). Ed Welch, in his book *When People Are Big and God Is Small*,[8] says fear of man has many symptoms: susceptibility to peer pressure; "needing" something from a spouse; a concern with self-esteem; being overcommitted because we can't say no; fear of being exposed; small lies to make ourselves look good; people making us jealous, angry, depressed, or anxious; avoiding people; comparing ourselves with others; and fear of evangelism.[9]

Our culture tries to overcome this problem by finding ways to bolster self-esteem. But this actually compounds the problem. We become dependent on whatever or whoever will boost our self-esteem. In reality, low self-esteem is thwarted pride: we don't have the status we think we deserve. We elevate desires that are often good in themselves (a desire for love, affirmation, or respect) to the level of needs without which we think we cannot be whole. We talk of "needing" the approval or acceptance of others, but our true need is to glorify God and love people.

The answer to the fear of man is fear of God. We need a big view of God. To fear God is to respect, worship, trust, and submit to him. It's the proper response to his glory, holiness, power, love, goodness, and wrath. The appearances of God are often described in the Bible in terms of brightness, fire, and brilliance. Think of the heat of the sun, with nuclear reactions within it creating a blinding brilliance even millions of miles away. Yet there's an intensity and substance to God's glory far beyond that of our sun. God wraps majesty and splendor around him like a cloak (Psalm 93:1). "To whom then will you compare me, that I should be like him? says the Holy One" (Isaiah 40:25). For the Christian, the fear of God no longer involves terror. He's our Father, and we come before him with confidence through Christ (Hebrews 4:14–16). But we can never get chummy with him. He remains a consuming fire. "My flesh trembles for fear of you," says the psalmist. "I am afraid of your judgments" (Psalm 119:120).

So, if you are controlled by people's expectations, then you need to learn the fear of the Lord, for the fear of God can be taught and learned (Deuteronomy 4:10; 17:18–19; 31:12; Psalm 34:9–11). Meditate on God's glory, greatness, holiness, power, splendor, beauty, grace, mercy, and love. Often, in Psalms 18 and 34, for example, this is what the psalmist is doing. In the face of some threat, he's speaking the truth about God to himself. He's reminding himself of God's glory so that fear of others is replaced by trust in God. Whenever you see someone whom you fear or whose approval you crave, imagine God next to him or her. Which of them is more glorious, majestic, holy, beautiful, threatening, and loving? Whose approval really matters to you? "Do not fear those who kill the body but cannot kill the soul," says Jesus. "Rather fear him who can destroy both soul and body in hell" (Matthew 10:28). Fear in the face of a threat is natural. But natural fear needs to be regulated by faith in God. Your boss may be a bully, but he or she isn't bigger than God. David had good cause to fear others at various points in his life, but he could say:

> The LORD is my light and my salvation;
> whom shall I fear?
> The LORD is the stronghold of my life;
> of whom shall I be afraid?
> (Psalm 27:1–3; see also Psalm 56:3–4)

The fear of God is liberating. We take people's expectations seriously because we want to love them as God commanded. But we're not enslaved by them. We don't serve them for what they can give us in return—approval, affection, security, or whatever. By submitting to Christ's lordship, we're free to serve others in love (Galatians 5:13).

3. God Is Good—So We Do Not Have to Look Elsewhere

I recently heard the story of an elderly widow in Russia who has taken a job cleaning the stairwells of a grim apartment block. Her state pension covers her own needs, but she wants to earn extra money for missionaries working in Mongolia. What makes someone do that for people and churches she'll never see in this life? The answer is joy. She is like the man who finds treasure in a field and "in his joy goes and sells all he has and buys that field" (Matthew 13:44). The invitation of the Bible is not to dreary abstinence. It's a call to find in God that which truly satisfies. It's believing that we find lasting fulfillment, satisfaction, joy, and identity in knowing God, and nowhere else. Whatever sin offers, God offers more, for God offers us himself. God isn't just good, he's better—better than everything else—and the true source of all joy.

In John 4, Jesus turns a request for water from a Samaritan woman into an offer of living water. "Everyone who drinks of this water will be thirsty again, but whoever drinks of the water that I will give him will never be thirsty again. The water that I will give him will become in him a spring of water welling up to eternal life" (vv. 13–14). This living water is God himself communicated to his people through the Holy Spirit (John 7:37–39). Every longing in us is a version of our longing for God. That longing may be a distorted version of our longing for God, but it's still a longing for the God we were made to know.

One of our problems is that we think only of moments. In the moment, we think the pleasures of sin are real and the joy of God is insubstantial or distant. But in truth it's the other way around: every joy we experience is but a shadow of the source of all joy, which is God. Marriage, for example, is a reflection of the joy of union with God, adultery a distorted reflection. If you idolize marriage or commit adultery, then you've settled for less than living water. Sin is like the distorted reflection of a beautiful sunset that shifts with every movement of the breeze across the water. God is the sun itself in all its beauty and glory and energy. C. S. Lewis says, "There have been times when I think we do not desire heaven; but more often I find myself wondering whether, in our hearts of hearts, we have ever desired anything else. . . . It is the secret signature of each soul, the incommunicable and unappeasable want."[10]

This is why nothing but God satisfies—only he satisfies in a true and lasting way. If you look for satisfaction or fulfillment, meaning or identity, anywhere other than in Jesus, you'll be left empty. There may be a moment of refreshment or pleasure, but you'll soon be thirsty again. Jesus asks the woman to fetch her husband. This looks like a tangent, but in fact it leads straight to her heart. The truth is that she's had five husbands and the man she's now with is not her husband. She's been looking for meaning, satisfaction, and fulfillment in marriage, sex, and intimacy. But they're like water that leaves her thirsty again. No doubt there was real pleasure. But it didn't last. It wasn't the real thing. It left her thirsty.

There was a clear pattern in her life. The math tells the story: five husbands plus another man.

What are the patterns in your life? Are the words "If only . . ." a refrain? What comes after the "If only . . ."? Do you really believe God is good?

When the woman tries to draw Jesus into worship controversies, Jesus redefines worship (vv. 19–24). Worship is not about location. It's an attitude of the heart: you worship in spirit and in truth. Worship is about what you desire most, what you think has most worth. Every time you look to God to satisfy your longings, you worship him in spirit and truth. Every time you look elsewhere, you commit idolatry. Even our good works can be idolatrous acts. If we don't delight in God for his own sake, finding him beautiful and glorious in our eyes, then we'll serve him for what we get in return: reputation, security, escape from hell. In so doing, we reveal that our greatest love is our reputation, our security, our self-preservation, ourselves.[11]

It's easy for us to think of obedience as the price we pay for entry into heaven. It would be better for us, we suppose, to be living for pleasure, but as Christians we have to live for God. But the life of obedience is not the bad or sad life. It's the good life. Life with God and for God is the best life you could live. Change is about *enjoying the freedom from sin and the delight in God that God gives to us through Jesus.*

> *Change is about enjoying the freedom from sin and the delight in God that God gives to us through Jesus.*

God is not only better than anything sin offers—God *is forever.* The Bible talks about the "pleasures of sin," and there's no doubt many sins do bring pleasure. There's no point pretending otherwise. But the Bible also tells us that the pleasures of sin are only for "a short time" (Hebrews 11:25, NIV).

> By faith Moses, when he was grown up, refused to be called the son of Pharaoh's daughter, choosing rather to be mistreated with the people of God than to enjoy the fleeting pleasures of sin. He considered the reproach of Christ greater wealth than the treasures of Egypt, for he was looking to the reward. (Hebrews 11:24–26)

We're called to look beyond the present moment to eternity. "The wages of sin," says Paul, "is death" (Romans 6:23). There is always a price to pay. Often those consequences are in this life: broken relationships, damaged bodies, a shamed conscience, addictive habits. Always there are consequences for the life to come. "Sin when it is fully grown," says James, "brings forth death" (James

1:15). We often focus on the temptation. It starts to fill our minds, and we lose sight of the bigger picture. One person I know broke the cycle of sin he was caught up in after visiting a Christian friend who was dying in a hospice. Suddenly he was confronted with the bigger picture and forced to look beyond his sin.

Think about Moses. We know from the pyramids and sphinxes that Egyptian rulers were extremely wealthy. This was as good as it got anywhere on earth at that time—the equivalent of today's multi-millionaire lifestyle. As a child of the royal court, Moses had it all. But he gave it all up, choosing to be ill-treated with the Hebrew slaves. This was because he recognized that Christ was better than all the treasures of Egypt. The Egyptians locked up their treasures in pyramids in an attempt to take them with them into the afterlife. But they couldn't do it. In fact, many of their treasures ended up in the British Museum. Moses, however, "was looking [ahead] to the reward." He realized that what God offered for all eternity was better by far than anything sin could offer in this life (Mark 8:34–36).

G. K. Chesterton suggests that at present we pursue variety because we're so easily wearied. But what if a man's "life and joy were so gigantic that he never tired of routine?"

> A child kicks his legs rhythmically through excess, not absence, of life. Because children have abounding vitality, because they are in spirit fierce and free, therefore they want things repeated and unchanged. They always say, "Do it again." . . . Perhaps God is strong enough to exult in monotony. It is possible that God says every morning, "Do it again" to the sun; and every evening, "Do it again" to the moon. It may not be automatic necessity that makes all daisies alike; it may be that God makes every daisy separately, but he has never got tired of making them. It may be that He has the eternal appetite of infancy; for we have sinned and grown old, and our Father is younger than we. The repetition in Nature may not be a mere recurrence; it may be a theatrical encore.[12]

We so easily grow bored with life. We are weary with sin-induced futility. But God is never bored by life. He *is* life. His joy and life are so gigantic that he never tires of sunrises and daisies, of beauty and life and joy. In Proverbs 8:30–31, Jesus, personified as Wisdom, speaks of his delight and joy in creation. Jesus says, in effect, "I was filled with fresh delight day after day, always laughing in God's presence, playing in every corner of his world and delighting in humanity."[13] We worry that eternity will be boring. But that is because we are dead and tired. We look for joy in sin, and we are quickly bored and always moving on in search of more. We grow weary in our futile pursuit of ever-greater excitement. But in eternity there will be a rush to life running through our veins. Our life and joy will be gigantic, so that each moment will bring fresh ecstasy; each daisy will be a fresh delight, each sunrise a fresh wonder. We will cry to God, "Again, again, do it again." Now we are old and tired and cynical. But then we will be young again, forever young, forever delighting in God.

4. God Is Gracious — So We Do Not Have to Prove Ourselves

I lay awake long into the night, replaying the conversation in my mind. The next morning the brooding continued. Our team meeting had developed into what my daughter later described as "war." Same place, same time, but the night before that, a woman in our church had come to me with a profound pastoral crisis. That night I'd slept soundly.

How crazy! I could forget a genuine crisis, happy to leave it in God's hands. But an argument about nothing had totally preoccupied me. My desire to be vindicated had consumed me. That's why I'd played a role in creating the conflict in the first place. I wanted to be proved right, so I fought on. What set me free from my self-centered brooding was the truth that God is gracious. I didn't need to justify myself. I *couldn't* justify myself. But God graciously justifies me through the finished work of Christ. God is "ready to forgive, gracious and merciful, slow to anger and abounding in steadfast love" (Nehemiah 9:17).

The parable of the prodigal son in Luke 15 reveals the remarkable grace of God. Asking for his inheritance was tantamount to the younger brother saying to his father, "I wish you were dead." Selling off that inheritance was shameful because it meant losing the family's land. Moving to another city was a rejection of his family. And we haven't even got to the wild living yet! Feeding pigs was as low as you could go for a good Jew, because pigs were unclean. And as for wanting to eat their food . . . ! This son is a picture of you and me. We've wished God dead, rejected his love, moved as far from God as we can. We've tried to break free from love and ended up in the pigsty, longing to be satisfied with rubbish.

But the gracious behavior of the father is even more shocking. This would have left Jesus' hearers gasping. If a son asked his father for his inheritance while the father was still alive, he would be disinherited. If a son tried to break free of his father's rule, he'd be beaten. If a son left home to indulge in wild living, he'd be disowned. But this father runs to meet his returning son. He doesn't wait for his son to honor him. He honors the son with a robe, a ring, and a party. This is our God—embracing, welcoming, and honoring us.

I used to think that when I let God down I would probably have a bad day or my prayers would go unanswered. I assumed God would act in the way I act when people let me down, giving them the cold shoulder. Or I thought I could atone by having a miserable day or sweating it out in prayer, as if the death of Jesus didn't quite do the job. And so we stand at a distance from God. And all the time he's looking for us, ready to embrace us, ready to welcome us home. Indeed, as the other parables of Luke 15 remind us, he takes the initiative to bring us home.

If the story of the younger brother reveals God's grace, in the older son we see many characteristics of not truly believing God is gracious.

Restless Anger

The older brother "was angry and refused to go in" (Luke 15:28). He's angry because the younger brother is being honored, as if he's in the right. All the older brother's hard work seems to count for nothing. That's the scandal of God's grace. Without grace, we view life as a contract between us and God: we do good works, and in return he blesses us. When things go well, we're filled with pride. But when things go badly, either we blame ourselves (and feel guilty) or we blame God (and feel bitter). Because we often leave God out of our explanations, this anger against God often feels ill-defined: we're not even sure why we're angry. But in actuality the contract or covenant between us and God already reads "Paid in full by the blood of Jesus." Only when we grasp God's grace are we free to serve him for his own sake, not for reward.

Joyless Duty

"All these years I've been slaving for you" (v. 29, NIV). The older son doesn't say he's been serving, partnering, or working with his father but "slaving." Imagine a woman who cooks for an ungrateful and unkind family. For her, work is drudgery. Now imagine a young bride whose husband is attentive, kind, and loving. Whatever she serves up, he thinks it is wonderful. Does she find her work drudgery? Joyless duty will characterize our attitude if we think of God as an uncaring boss. But when we see him as a gracious Father, our attitude will be one of joyful service.

Anxious Performance

"I never disobeyed your command" (v. 29). The older brother wants people to know about his good works because he's trying to prove himself. There are people trying to perform day after day—Christian leaders trying to preach a wonderful sermon every week, parents trying to produce lovely children, workers putting in long hours at work, all in a desperate attempt to prove themselves. And some weeks they may feel as if they've pulled it off. And other weeks it all seems so fragile, as if it might shatter. And so they live in a constant state of stress and busyness, always striving to put in another great performance, always worried that the charade might crumble. We can't justify ourselves, and we don't have to! God is gracious: he throws his arms around us.

Proud Comparisons

"This son of yours . . . has devoured your property with prostitutes" (v. 30). This is the first mention of prostitutes. But the older brother assumes the worst in order to paint his brother in the worst possible light. Or we disguise pride as kindness and patronize people. We highlight other people's faults so we can look better. We think of righteousness as a ladder, and our position on the ladder is what matters.

But God's grace turns our assessments on their head. We stand together at the foot of the cross—equally ashamed, equally accepted. Jesus tells the parable of the prodigal because the Pharisees are muttering about the way he welcomes sinners and eats with them (vv. 1–2). It turns out that God isn't interested in respectability or self-righteousness. He's interested in returning sinners. Jesus is right to party with notorious sinners because heaven is a party for sinners (vv. 7, 10, 21–24).

Many of us are confident we'll be justified on the last day: acquitted before God through the death of Jesus. But what about justification today and tomorrow? Are you still trying to prove yourself?

- Do you ever get angry or brood because you want to prove you're in the right?
- Does your Christian service feel like joyless duty?
- Do you ever feel the pressure to perform?
- Do you serve others so you can feel good about yourself or impress people?
- Do you look down on others or exaggerate their failings?
- Do you worry that you won't make the grade in life?
- Do you enjoy conversations about the shortcomings of others?

The older son doesn't see himself as a son at all but as a servant. The father has his obedience, but not his love. Does God the Father have your obedience, but not your love?

Here's the shocking truth: without justifying faith people "never do anything out of love to God, but only out of self-love or fear of damnation."[14] There are acts that look like good works, but in fact they reflect a belief that the best way to get into God's good books or to prove myself to others is through what I do. I declare myself to be a better savior than Jesus.[15] We think we must finish off what Christ left undone. That's why Jesus says, "This is the work of God, that you believe in him whom he has sent" (John 6:29). There's only one thing God wants us to do: have faith in his Son. Everything else will flow from that.

Let me repeat the words of William Romaine: "No sin can be crucified either in heart or life unless it first be pardoned in conscience. . . . If it be not mortified in its guilt, it cannot be subdued in its power."[16] Richard Lovelace claims the main reason Christians do not change is a failure really to grasp God's grace:

> Christians who are no longer sure that God loves and accepts them in Jesus, apart from their present spiritual achievements, are subconsciously radically insecure persons. . . . Their insecurity shows itself in pride, a fierce defensive assertion of their own righteousness and defensive criticism of others. . . . They cling desperately to legal, pharisaical righteousness, but envy, jealousy and other branches of the tree of sin grow out of their fundamental insecurity.[17]

All is not lost. The father goes out to plead with the older brother (Luke 15:28). He welcomes his dissolute son, and he welcomes his self-righteous son. At the end of the story the older brother is still on the outside of the party. We're left wondering what he'll do. It forces us to wonder what *we* would do—what we *will* do. Will we live believing that God is gracious?

In the temple the work of atonement was never done. The priests were at it day after day (Hebrews 10:11). But Jesus has sat down (v. 12). He's done all that's required. And so we can sit down too. We don't have to be up and busy making atonement, proving ourselves, earning God's blessing, performing.

View him prostrate in the garden,
On the ground your Maker lies.
Then on Calvary's tree behold him,
Hear him cry before he dies:
"It is finished! It is finished!"
Sinner, will not this suffice?[18]

Conclusion

We can sin only if we suffer from a radical loss of perspective. Only if we forget that God is great and good can we sin. But that is what we do time after time. We forget our God and the identity he gives. Change takes place through faith in our great and good God. It takes place as we preach truth to our hearts. This doesn't mean it's easy. We just have to believe, but that's a big *just*! Faith is a daily struggle. Lies about God are all around us: the world, the flesh and the devil whisper them constantly to our hearts. It's a struggle. But it's also possible. "This is the victory that has overcome the world—our faith" (1 John 5:4).

What does this mean in practice? First, we need to nurture our trust in God's greatness, our fear of God's glory, our delight in God's goodness, our longing for God's future, our rest in God's grace. We need to do this day by day through the Word, prayer, and the Christian community (more of this in chapter 9).

Second, when we face temptation we need to say not only "I should not do this," but also "I need not do this." When tempted to envy another's possession, we say not only "I must not envy," but also "I need not envy because I have Christ." When tempted to worry, we say not only "I must not worry," but "I need not worry because God is in control." Whatever sin offers, God is bigger and better.

To say to temptation, "I must not do this" is legalism. To say, "I need not do this because God is bigger and better" is good news.

Reflection

1. What might be the lies behind the following behaviors or emotions? There may well be several possible answers. What truths do each of these people need to turn to in faith?

Abdul often complains. He's been ill for years, and the doctors aren't really sure what's wrong. It gets him down, and it's all he can ever talk about.

Colin's tired, so tired he often loses patience with the children, and last night, when his wife wanted to talk to him, he fell asleep on the sofa. He's working all the overtime he can get. He wants to be a good provider for his family, but it's a struggle meeting the mortgage payments.

Cathy is thinking of moving in with her boyfriend. Her Christian friends tell her it's wrong. But they don't appreciate the way Paul makes her feel loved. She felt so empty before Paul came into her life, and now she feels kind of complete. Besides, it's easy for them, as they're mostly married.

Jamal spends hours on computer games. It's damaging his relationships with his family. He's not really living up to his responsibilities. Real life is a bit boring, for he's just an ordinary guy. But in the virtual world he's a hero.

Every morning Elsa feels the tension in her stomach as she sets off for school. Her classmates bad-mouth their teachers and gossip about others. They obsess about the latest fashions and the boys they're going out with. Every now and then they make fun of Elsa for not really joining in. Sometimes she does things she knows are wrong. Most of the time she just feels on the edge.

Carla often gossips about people. She loves to put them down and point out their faults. It makes her feel good about herself.

2. Write a version of Psalm 27 in which you make it say the opposite of what it actually says. For example:

The Lord is my light and my salvation —
whom shall I fear?

My spouse lights up my life —
I crave her approval.

The Lord is the stronghold of my life —
of whom shall I be afraid?

My boss guarantees my security —
I'm afraid of upsetting him.

When evil men advance against me to
    devour my flesh,
when my enemies and my foes attack me,
they will stumble and fall.

When my peers turn against me,
when they mock me,
I stumble and fall.

How much of your opposite version reflects the way you actually think at times? What are the corresponding truths from the real version of the Psalm that counter this wrong thinking about God?

Repeat the exercise with Psalms 31, 84, and 103.

Change Project

What truths do you need to turn to?

What thoughts are behind your behavior or emotions?

Think about the issue you've identified in your change project.

- Why do you do or feel what you do or feel?
- What do you hope to achieve?
- What do you think will make you happy in that situation?
- What beliefs or thoughts shape your behavior or emotions?

What's the lie?
Behind every sin and every negative emotion is a lie. What's the lie behind the issue you've chosen for your change project?

What do your thoughts show about your trust in God?
It's important to express your beliefs or thoughts as beliefs or thoughts about God. We don't often do this. We leave God out of the picture. As a result, we don't see our thoughts as lies about God. Restate your thinking, with God included. The following questions may help:

- If you want something, do you think it offers more than God offers?
- If you fear something, do you think it is more important than God?
- If you're angry about something, do you feel that God has let you down?

What truths do you need to turn to?
Turn the answer to your previous question the opposite way around. *If this is the lie, what is the truth?* Which of the following

truths particularly apply to the lies behind the area you have chosen in your change project?

- God is great—so we do not have to be in control.
- God is glorious—so we do not have to fear others.
- God is good—so we do not have to look elsewhere.
- God is gracious—so we do not have to prove ourselves.

The following passages of Scripture talk about these truths. Meditate on them. Turn them into prayer. Ask God to help you remember them and believe them in moments of temptation.

- God is great—Psalm 27.
- God is glorious—Psalm 31.
- God is good—Psalm 94.
- God is gracious—Psalm 103.

Write a summary of the truths you need to turn to in faith.

CHAPTER SIX

WHAT DESIRES DO YOU NEED TO TURN FROM?

"**Preparing your minds for action,** and being sober-minded, set your hope fully on the grace that will be brought to you at the revelation of Jesus Christ. As obedient children, do not be conformed to the passions of your former ignorance, but as he who called you is holy, you also be holy in all your conduct" (1 Peter 1:13–15).

God's agenda for our lives is for us to be holy, just as he is holy. This holiness is the fruit of what we think or trust and what we desire or worship. We've seen that sinful behavior and negative emotions arise when we believe lies about God instead of trusting God's Word. So Peter tells us to "prepare [our] minds for action." We're to fill our minds with truth and battle with our unbelieving thoughts. Peter also tells us not to "conform to the passions" we had when in our "former ignorance" (see also 1 Peter 2:11). The other thing going on in our hearts is that we desire, worship, and treasure. We sin because we desire or worship idols instead of worshipping God.

We Desire or Worship Idols Instead of Worshipping God

We don't often think of ourselves as worshipping idols because we think of idols in terms of statues and shrines. But God tells the leaders of Israel that they "have taken their idols into their hearts" (Ezekiel 14:3). We shouldn't look down on the Israelites for worshipping idols. We should instead see a mirror of our own hearts.

John Calvin says, "Man's nature, so to speak, is a perpetual factory of idols."[1] God says, "My people have committed two evils: they have forsaken me, the fountain of living waters, and hewed cisterns for themselves, broken cisterns that can hold no water." As a result, they "go after other gods to [their] own harm" and "to their own shame" (Jeremiah 2:13; 7:6, 19). An idol is anything we look to instead of God for living water. Our double sin is, first, rejecting the truth of God's greatness and goodness and, second, placing our affections elsewhere.

> A god is whatever we expect to provide all good and in which we take refuge in all distress. . . . Whatever you set your heart on and put your trust in, that, I tell you, is your true god. (Martin Luther)[2]

> Idolatry may not involve explicit denials of God's existence or character. It may well come in the form of an over-attachment to something that is, in itself, perfectly good. . . . An idol can be a physical object, a property, a person, an activity, a role, an institution, a hope, an image, an idea, a pleasure, a hero—anything that can substitute for God. (Richard Keyes)[3]

> *Our idols are those things we count on to give our lives meaning.* They are the things of which we say, "I need this to make me happy," or "If I don't have this my life is worthless and meaningless." (Tim Keller)[4]

The New Testament way of talking about idolatry is "sinful desires." Literally, it is "the lusts of the flesh." "Lusts" here is not just sexual desire, but all sinful desire. And "flesh" is not talking about our bodies, but about our sinful natures—the bias toward sin that we have from birth. Paul describes "covetousness" or greed as "idolatry" (Colossians 3:5). Your idol is whatever you're greedy for. It may be money, approval, sex, or power. David Powlison says, "If 'idolatry' is the characteristic and summary Old Testament word for our drift from God, then 'desires' is the characteristic and summary New Testament word for the same drift. Both are shorthand for the problem of human beings."[5] In other words, "sinful desires of the flesh" is another way of talking about the idols of the heart. Tim Stafford says:

> The "flesh"—that is, our lives without God—urgently desires many things. It wants power. It wants pleasure. It wants wealth. It wants status and admiration. None of these is wrong in itself. And nothing would be wrong with liking these things. But desire, or lust, is more than liking. It is the will to possess. Lust turns good things into objects of worship. And that is why lust, or covetousness, is so closely linked to another biblical word: idolatry. What we lust for we worship. We may joke about our lusts, but our behavior shows a more fundamental allegiance. We look to our idols to give us what we need—to make our lives rich and purposeful.[6]

We think we're free when we break away from God, but we become enslaved by our own sinful desires.

"For where your treasure is," says Jesus, "there your heart will be also" (Matthew 6:21). Whatever you treasure most is the thing that has your heart and controls your life. The process is described well by our English word *captivated*. We're made captive by our desires. Our hearts are captured. We confuse free-willed with self-willed. We think we're free when we break away from God, but we become enslaved by our own sinful desires. "Whatever overcomes a person, to that he is enslaved" (2 Peter 2:19). "No one can serve two masters, for either he will hate the one and love the other, or he will be devoted to the one and despise the other. You cannot serve God and money" (Matthew 6:24). We serve whatever our hearts desire most. If that desire is for God and his glory, then God is our master. But if our desire is, for example, for money, then money is our master, and that's idolatry.

"When the woman saw that the tree was good for food, and

that it was a delight to the eyes, and that the tree was to be desired to make one wise, she took of its fruit and ate, and she also gave some to her husband who was with her, and he ate" (Genesis 3:6). "Good . . . delight . . . desired." Elyse Fitzpatrick comments, "Our choices are predicated upon what we think is 'good,' what we 'delight in,' what we find most 'desirable.' The truth about our choices is that we always choose what we believe to be our best. We always choose what we believe will bring us the most delight."[7] Eve thought the fruit could give her more than God, and so she desired the fruit. That desire controlled her heart and determined her behavior. This was true of the first sin, and it's true of all subsequent sin. "Each person is tempted when he is lured and enticed by his own desire. Then desire when it has conceived gives birth to sin, and sin when it is fully grown brings forth death" (James 1:14–15). Sin begins with desire. We're not sinners because we commit sinful acts. We commit sinful acts because we're sinners, born with a bias to sin, enslaved by our sinful desires. That's why we can't change ourselves simply by changing our behavior. We need God to change us by renewing our hearts and giving us new desires.

Every sin begins in the heart with a sinful desire. "God gave them up in the lusts of their hearts to impurity, to the dishonoring of their bodies among themselves, because they exchanged the truth about God for a lie and worshiped and served the creature rather than the Creator, who is blessed forever! Amen" (Romans 1:24–25). We've seen how sin arises because we exchange the truth about God for a lie. Now we see that sin also arises because God gives us over to the sinful desires of our hearts. It arises when we worship or desire created things rather than the Creator. Our double problem is that we believe lies rather than believing God (chapter 5) and worship idols rather than worshipping God (chapter 6, our current study).

Desire is at the helm of our lives. It determines our behavior. *We always do what we want to do.* The question is, which of our desires is strongest at any given moment? An alcoholic may desire or want a drink but refrains from having one. It looks as if he's not doing what he wants. But what has happened is that another desire (perhaps the desire to avoid shame or losing his family) has trumped the desire for a drink. He's still doing what he wants; it's just that the desire for a drink is no longer his biggest desire.[8] We excuse ourselves by thinking that we want to be good but are the victims of other factors (circumstances, history, biology, ill health, and so on). But the Bible's radical view of sin tells us that we are responsible. We always do what we want to do.

But this also gives us hope. In Romans 7, Paul describes someone who says, "For I do not do the good I want, but the evil I do not want is what I keep on doing" (v. 19). At first sight this might seem to contradict what we've been saying. Here is someone who doesn't do what he wants to do. But the reason he doesn't follow his good desires is that his sinful desires are stronger and therefore controlling (Romans 1:24–26; 7:23–25). The answer is, says Paul, the Holy Spirit and the new desires he gives:

> Those who live according to the sinful nature have their minds set on what that nature desires; but those who live in accordance with the Spirit have their minds set on what the Spirit desires. . . . Those controlled by the sinful nature cannot please God. You, however, are controlled not by the sinful nature but by the Spirit, if the Spirit of God lives in you. (Romans 8:5, 8–9, NIV)

This understanding humbles us, but it also gives us hope for change. We are changed by faith as we look upon the glory of God and so find him more desirable than anything sin might offer. By faith and through the Spirit, the desire for God trumps the desire for sin.

When Desires Go Bad

Desire itself isn't wrong. Desire is part of being human. We should desire God and his glory (Luke 22:15; 1 Corinthians 12:31). A sinful desire is a desire that is bigger than God. It could be a desire for *a good thing that has become more important to us than God.* The word translated "sinful desires" is *epithumiai*, or "over-desires." To paraphrase Calvin: "Our problem is not the natural desires God wrote into our character at creation, the desires [for love, for order, for pleasure] that make us human. Our problem is desires which struggle against God's control. . . . Human desires are evil and sinful, not because we desire unnatural things, but because our desires are inordinate."[9] It's not usually the thing we want that is the problem, but that we want it more than God. To want to be married or successful or healthy, for example, is to desire a good thing. But if my singleness or failure or illness makes me bitter, then my desire has grown too big, bigger than my desire for God. As a result, I cannot be content with God's sovereignty over my life.

The world is full of good things given by God. We can, and indeed should, enjoy them. But they're meant as bridges to joy in God. We delight in the gift and the Giver. We do this by receiving them with thanksgiving. "For everything created by God is good, and nothing is to be rejected if it is received with thanksgiving, for it is made holy by the word of God and prayer" (1 Timothy 4:4–5). But a good thing can become a "god-thing" if it eclipses God, if the gift matters more to us than the Giver.

In John 6 Jesus miraculously feeds five thousand men (plus women and children) with just five loaves and two fish. The next day the crowd come, wanting more. Here are people who come to Jesus looking for satisfaction. What could be wrong with that? But they're not interested in Jesus—they simply want a free meal. "Jesus answered them, 'Truly, truly, I say to you, you are seeking me, not because you saw signs, but because you ate your fill of the loaves'" (v. 26). Jesus urges them not to look to him to fulfill their idolatrous desires, but to find the true satisfaction that he offers. "Do not labor for the food that perishes, but for the food that endures to eternal life, which the Son of Man will give to you" (v. 27). They want Jesus to meet their immediate desires.

It can be the same with us. We look to God to provide our material and emotional needs. And often he does. But God always has a bigger agenda. He wants us to know him and serve him. He wants us to become like his Son. When our desires grow more important to us than Jesus, then God will stick to his bigger agenda.

"The heart is deceitful above all things" (Jeremiah 17:9). The lusts of the heart are "deceitful desires" (Ephesians 4:22). One common way desires deceive us is by masquerading as needs. We don't say, "I lust to be loved"; we say, "I need to be loved." We take a good desire (to be loved) and turn it into an idolatrous desire and call it a need. God and his glory are then no longer at the center of my outlook. Instead I'm at the center, demanding that people "worship" me by giving me affection and affirmation. Richard Lovelace calls it our "god complex."[10]

God promises to meet our true needs, but we can't expect him to satisfy our selfish desires. God isn't a divine waiter, ready to serve us whatever we want. God isn't the key to the good life (however I choose to define it). He defines the good life. He *is* the good life. God must be desired for his own sake, not as the purveyor of worldly success.

Carolyn wanted a husband and was looking to God to provide one. She had tried to live a godly life, but God, she claimed, hadn't kept his side of the bargain. And so she was angry at him. In the course of several conversations, I spoke of God's grace. But talk of grace didn't bring change to Carolyn's life. What I didn't see at the time was that there was a bigger, more fundamental problem in her heart. Carolyn's desire for a husband had become an idol. She wanted a husband more than she wanted God. So when God didn't provide one, she became bitter toward him. What I should have said to her was, "'Taste and see that the LORD is good' [Psalm 34:8]. Turn from your idolatry; find satisfaction in the Bread of Life, and you will never be hungry."

In Amos 4 God speaks of a gift he gave to his people: "empty stomachs" (v. 6, NIV). He "withheld rain" so that "people staggered from town to town for water" (vv. 7–8, NIV). He struck their crops with mildew (v. 9). These might seem strange gifts! But God gives them so that his people might repent. The gifts are terrible things, but idolatry and its consequences are worse. God always seeks the best for his people, and that best is himself. Famine and thirst are acts of divine love when their aim is to bring us back to God.

Repentance: Turning from Our Sinful Desires

Sin arises because we desire something more than we desire God. Overcoming sin begins by reversing this process: desiring God more than other things. The Bible calls this "repentance." That word means "turning": we turn away from our idolatrous desires and turn in faith toward God.

Sin arises because we desire something more than God. Overcoming sin begins by reversing this process: desiring God more than other things.

Sin is fundamentally an orientation toward self. We won't let God be God of our lives. We run our lives our way, without him. Self is at the center of the picture. Repentance is reorienting ourselves toward God. It's putting God at the center. What matters most is no longer our pleasure or success or even our problems, but God's glory (2 Corinthians 12:7–9).

Our problem is that we think of ourselves as being at the center of our world. We think of our lives as a story and, if we're Christians, God is one of the characters in our story. We look for him when we need him and expect him to be grateful when we serve him. He's a lovely piece of our story, but we still think of it as our story. But it's not our story. It's God's story. Of course there is a sense in which God is there for us. But the bigger reality is that we're there for God. We exist to give him glory. He doesn't owe us anything, not even explanations. Meanwhile, we owe him everything as our Creator and Redeemer.

It's so much better to be a minor character in God's story than to try to write our own script. Living with God at the center is the good and sane life. It's better to enjoy the warmth of the sun than to light a bonfire in our home. It's better to reflect the glory of God than to be consumed by the empty pursuit of our own glory.

One of my recurrent sins is self-pity. If someone treats me badly, I get in a huff. If something goes wrong, I'm grumpy. I can just wake up in a dark mood. I act as if I'm all that matters in my life, as if I'm the axis on which my world spins. But I'm not. I was made to glorify God and enjoy him forever. I may need to give myself a stiff talking to, but there's such freedom in accepting that this is God's world, not mine. I'm grumpy because things aren't going my way. But I've no right and no need to expect them to go my way. It's enough to know that they're going God's way and that his ways are good.

This new God-centered perspective is both humbling and liberating. It's humbling because it puts us in our place. We're not the center of the world. We're not even the center of our world. But it's also liberating. We no longer need to try continually to be in control. We can let God be God. Our reputation is no longer what matters. We're no longer controlled by the approval or rejection of others. We're free to serve others in love.

Continual Repentance

We become Christians through faith and repentance, and we grow as Christians through continual faith and repentance. We don't graduate from the gospel to some advanced way of holiness or progress. Martin Luther said, "To progress is always to begin again."[11]

So repentance is not a one-time event that just takes place when we're converted. John Calvin says, "God assigns to [believers] a race of repentance, which they are to run throughout their lives."[12] Repentance is a lifelong, continuous activity of turning back to God from God-dethroning desires. And repentance is not just turning from sinful behavior, but turning from the idols and desires that cause sinful behavior.

One way in which the Bible describes the ongoing activity of repentance is the imagery of mortification. This means putting sin to death. "Put to death therefore what is earthly in you: sexual immorality, impurity, passion, evil desire, and covetousness, which is idolatry" (Colossians 3:5). It means constantly saying a decisive no to sin in our lives, especially at the earliest stages of temptation.

Sin is mortified in our lives *through Christ* and *by the Spirit*. The foundation of mortification is Christ's work on the cross. "We know that our old self was crucified with [Christ] in order that the body of sin might be brought to nothing, so that we would no longer be enslaved to sin" (Romans 6:6; see also Galatians 2:20; 5:24). Christ dealt a fatal blow to our old sinful nature on the cross, freeing us from its power. It's because we "died . . . with Christ" and "have been raised with Christ" that we're to "put to death . . . what is earthly in [us]" (Colossians 2:20; 3:1, 5). We do this in the power of the Spirit: "if by the Spirit you put to death the deeds of the body, you will live" (Romans 8:13). The Spirit gives us a new heart with new God-glorifying desires. Repentance (turning from sinful desires) or mortification (killing off sinful desires) is Christ's work for us and the Spirit's work in us. But with the Spirit's help, we are active participants in the process.

Mortification is like gardening. We need to weed out the sin in our lives. My garden is plagued by different kinds of weeds. We've inherited some tree stumps. Removing them is hard work: you need a pickax, a whole afternoon, and my friend Steve. We also have a lot of scarlet pimpernel. That's easy to dig up, but neglect it for a few weeks and it'll quickly take over. We also have brambles. You can pull them up easily enough provided you wear thick gloves. But leave even a small piece of root in the ground and they'll come back.

Sometimes weeding out sin is like pulling up tree stumps. A particular sin may have gripped our heart for so long that its roots run deep. It's become a habit. Pulling up this weed will be hard and painful work. It's better by far to pull up the weeds of sin as soon as they emerge, when they're still small and rootless, like the scarlet pimpernel. But this is a constant task. Every day's neglect makes the job harder. The key thing is to mortify the roots of sin. We need to be putting to death sinful desires, not just changing our behavior. Otherwise sin will be like my brambles, growing again from any root left behind. Of course, I don't know where bramble roots are until they emerge from the ground, but when I see the shoots I can dig out the roots. When you see sinful behavior, follow it back to its root. Sinclair Ferguson says:

> What then is this killing of sin? It is the constant battle against sin which we fight daily—the refusal to allow the eye to wander, the mind to contemplate, the affections to run after anything which will draw us from Christ. It is the deliberate rejection of any sinful thought, suggestion, desire, aspiration, deed, circumstance or provocation at the moment we become conscious of its existence.[13]

"At the moment we become conscious of its existence." My problem is that I don't do this. A sinful desire gives rise to temptation, and I think, "I'm not actually sinning." So I play with the thought in my mind. I let my eyes linger. I let my mind wander. And so the desire grows. I feed it and encourage it and then complain that it's too strong. And all the time I am sinning—maybe not in my actions, but in my will, because I've not said no to sin.[14] We need to discipline our hearts to say no at the moment we become conscious of sinful desires.

I've found so much freedom simply by realizing that sinful desires are sinful.

- I feel myself getting bitter. Once I might have fed my desire by reflecting on all the wrongs I endure. But I realize now that bitterness is grumbling against God's goodness. And so (in my best moments and with God's help) I try to stop it before it grows.

- I feel myself getting annoyed. Once I might have fed my desire by reflecting on other people's incompetence. But I realize now that I get annoyed because of my desire to be in control instead of trusting God's sovereignty. And so I try to stop it before it grows.
- I feel myself getting angry. Once I might have fed my desire by reflecting on how I've been mistreated. But I realize now that I get angry because of my desire to justify myself instead of trusting in Christ's atoning work. And so I try to stop.

It's not necessarily wise to go on an idol hunt all the time or explore every motive. That might lead to unhealthy introspection. Our focus should be on God's liberating truth. A good guide is to explore your sinful desires only when you see the bad fruit of sinful behavior and negative emotions in your life.

People often ask me, "How can I tell whether a desire is sinful or not? How can I know whether I desire something too much?" I answer, by pointing to Jesus' image of bad fruit growing from a bad tree (Luke 6:43–45). You discover that a desire is sinful when it produces bad fruit in your life (disobedience, anger, anxiety, and so on). When you see that bad fruit, trace it back to the idolatrous desires of your heart.

Introspective self-analysis is a recent cultural phenomenon. Our evangelical forebears practiced self-examination, but it was different. They assumed a clear link between actions and the heart. Spotting that link was made difficult by the deceitfulness of sin, but the answer was not deep introspection but illumination brought by the Spirit and the Word. But we live in a post-Freud era. Sigmund Freud said that the roots of our actions and emotions are deep in our subconscious. Because they're subconscious, we need to dig them out by means of deep and endless introspection. We often bring this model to sanctification. We think we need some form of analysis or counseling to undercover the hidden depths of our actions. In reality, our need is to look to Christ. Dr. Martyn Lloyd-Jones writes, "We cross the line from self-examination to introspection when, in a sense, we do nothing but examine ourselves. . . . If we are always talking to people about ourselves and our problems . . . it probably means that we are all the time centered upon ourselves."[15]

Introspection assumes I'm what matters in sanctification. But it's God who changes us. Ask God to expose your heart by the Spirit through his Word (Psalm 139:23–24; Hebrews 4:12–13). But don't linger when looking at yourself. Linger when looking at Christ. As Robert Murray M'Cheyne famously said, "For one look at yourself, take ten looks at Christ."[16]

Along with weeding out sin, we need to plant in grace. When other plants are thriving, weeds grow poorly because they're deprived of space, light, water, and nutrients. It's the same with Christians. When our thoughts are filled with the glory of God and our lives are filled with the service of God, there'll be less room for sin and temptation (Galatians 6:7–10). (We'll come back to this in chapter 8.)

Creating Habits, Building Character

We can sometimes think that small concessions to temptation don't really matter: the lustful look, the resentful thoughts, the brief fantasy. They don't lead to anything, we tell ourselves. But small concessions don't satisfy temptation—*they fuel it!* Giving in to temptation makes temptation come more quickly and strongly next time. In time sin can become a habit. But turning from sin can also become a habit. Instead of temptation coming more quickly and strongly, it comes less often and less strongly. In moments of pressure, our minds go to God instead of to sin. Most of our moral decisions are reflex responses. We act in the moment. Before we know it, malicious words are out of our mouth, and we can't take them back. What counts in those situations isn't our ability to carry out moral reasoning or biblical reflection. It's the habit of holiness. It's Christian character. It's an undivided heart. The Victorian novelist Charles Reade said, "Sow an act, and you reap a habit. Sow a habit, and you reap a character. Sow a character, and you reap a destiny."

In 1569 Dirk Willems escaped from a Dutch prison. He'd been imprisoned because he was an Anabaptist, someone who believed the church was made up only of professing believers. Willems fled across a frozen lake, pursued by a prison guard. Half-starved from prison rations, Willems crossed the lake safely. But the guard fell through the ice into the freezing water. Willems immediately turned back and pulled him out. The guard wanted to release Willems, but by then a burgomaster had arrived on the scene. Willems was arrested, tortured, and burned at the stake. Willems didn't have time to decide on the right thing to do. He reacted in a moment. That's a sign of Christian character. It's a sign that grace has become a habit. You can't create Christian character overnight. It's the fruit of suffering and perseverance (Romans 5:3–4). It's the harvest of daily weeding out sin and planting grace. Paul Toews comments:

> For Mennonites no other story out of the sixteenth century has so captured the imagination. What Dirk did on that icy pond was reflexive—he didn't have to stop and think whether it was right or wrong or what the consequences would be. He simply did what his faith compelled him to do. Willems' spontaneous response to someone in need comes only from a heart undivided.[17]

What counts isn't our ability to carry out moral reasoning or biblical reflection. It's the habit of holiness. It's Christian character. It's an undivided heart.

We Repent by Faith: Believing God Is Bigger and Better than Our Sinful Desires

How do we repent? We repent through faith. We turn back to the worship of God when we believe that God is better than our idols.

In the past I've sometimes suspected that repentance was an add-on work: we're not really saved by faith alone, it turns out, but by faith plus repentance. But this isn't true. Turning to God in faith and turning from sin in repentance are the same movement. Try it now. Stand facing the window. Then turn to face the opposite wall. The act of turning from the window and the act of turning toward the wall is one movement. You can't turn toward the wall without turning away from the window. And you can't turn to God in faith without turning away from sin in repentance. When we trust God, we're affirming that he's bigger and better than our sinful desires. Repentance is in itself an act of faith.

God Is Bigger Than My Sinful Desires

Sometimes in the pressure of temptation we feel sin is inevitable. A friend once emailed me, "Temptation comes in two forms. 1. Sin seems attractive. 2. Sin seems inevitable. We feel like we can't do anything about it. We feel trapped. And so we give in to sin."

That's certainly true in my experience. I say no to temptation, but the temptation keeps coming back. In the end it no longer seems a question of whether I'll give in, but when. But this is a lie. Sin isn't inevitable for a child of God. We've been set free from its power. I need to believe the truth that God is bigger than my sinful desires. I need faith in God's power if I'm to repent of my sin.

God Is Better Than My Sinful Desires

We choose to follow our sinful desires because in that moment we believe they offer more than God. Faith is the realization that God is much, much better than my sinful desires. And when we affirm this in our hearts, we'll inevitably turn from those deceptive and empty desires to find true satisfaction in God.

> Why do you spend your money for that which is not bread,
> and your labor for that which does not satisfy?
> Listen diligently to me, and eat what is good,
> and delight yourselves in rich food. (Isaiah 55:2)

"O Israel, stay away from idols!
I am the one who answers your prayers and cares for you.
I am like a tree that is always green;
all your fruit comes from me." (Hosea 14:8, NLT)

Reflection

People tend to think of "sins" in the plural as consciously willed acts where one was aware of and chose not to do the righteous alternative. . . . But God's descriptions of sin often highlight the unconscious aspect. Sin—the desires we pursue, the beliefs we hold, the habits we obey as second nature—is intrinsically deceitful. If we knew we were deceived, we would not be deceived. But we are deceived, unless awakened through God's truth and Spirit. Sin is a darkened mind, drunkenness, animal-like instinct and compulsion, madness, slavery, ignorance, stupor. People often think that to define sin as unconscious removes human responsibility. How can we be culpable for what we did not sit down and choose to do?

But the Bible takes the opposite track. The unconscious and semi-conscious nature of much sin simply testifies to the fact that we are steeped in it. Sinners think, want, and act sin-like by nature, nurture, and practice. (David Powlison)[18]

Change Project

What desires do you need to turn from?

What are the idols of your heart?

- When you're angry, what are you not getting that you want?
- When you're anxious, what is threatened?
- When you're despondent, what have you lost or failed at?
- What do you think you need to have? "I'd be happy if only I could have . . ."

What desires control your heart?

Revisit the questions from chapter 4. Think about what is going on in your heart when you do or feel the area you've chosen in your change project.

- What did you want, desire, or wish for?
- What did you fear? What were you worrying about?
- What did you think you needed?
- What were your strategies and intentions designed to accomplish?
- What or whom were you trusting?
- Whom were you trying to please? Whose opinion of you counted?
- What were you loving? What were you hating?
- What would have brought you the greatest happiness, pleasure, or delight? What would have brought you the greatest pain and misery?[19]

Write a summary of the heart desires from which you need to turn.

CHAPTER SEVEN

WHAT STOPS YOU FROM CHANGING?

"I've tried changing, but I don't seem to get very far." "It's the same old story with the same old sin." "I could write the manual on holiness, but I still keep falling." "I've been working on my change project, but this week has put me back at square one." We've seen that God is at work changing us. So why don't we change more than we do? What stops us from changing? The more I've reflected on my own struggles, my experience as a pastor, and the Bible, the more persuaded I've become that it comes down to one of two things: a love of self or a love of sin. It's not lack of discipline or knowledge or support. These all matter, but the number-one reason why people don't change is pride, closely followed by hating the consequences of sin but actually still loving the sin itself.

Proud Self-reliance

Have you ever been frustrated or angry at your lack of change? Many people have said to me at some point, "I can't believe I've done it again," or "I'm so cross with myself for doing this." I've thought this many times myself. But listen to Ed Welch: "Perhaps the person is mad at himself for repeating the same sin over and over again. This is actually a veiled form of pride that assumes he is capable of doing good in his own power. He is minimizing his spiritual inability apart from God's grace."[1] Jerry Bridges claims, "God wants us to walk in obedience—not victory." Our problem, he explains, "is that our attitude toward sin is more self-centered than God-centered. We are more concerned about our own 'victory' over sin than we are about the fact that our sins grieve the heart of God."[2]

Pride isn't just a sin; it's part of the definition of sin. Pride puts us in the place of God. We turn from our chief end of glorying God and make our chief end glorifying ourselves. And we even do this with sanctification. We make sanctification our achievement and glory. C. J. Mahaney calls this "cosmic plagiarism."[3]

This is why humility is a paradigm of repentance. To humble ourselves before God is to repent of our god complex. This is why walking humbly before our God is what God requires (Micah 6:8). "[Scripture] says: 'God opposes the proud, but gives grace to the humble.' . . . Humble yourselves before the Lord, and he will exalt you" (James 4:6, 10; also 1 Peter 5:5). Humility is the secret to receiving grace. As Jack Miller says, "Grace flows downhill." People used to talk about the higher life of sanctification, but what we really need is the lower life. "We grow *up* into Christ by growing *down* into lowliness."[4] If we truly want the grace of holiness, we must get lower, humbling ourselves and leaving the lifting up to God.

> People used to talk about the higher life of sanctification, but what we really need is the lower life.

Humility, of course, isn't some spiritual achievement that merits God's grace. Quite the opposite. It's the realization that we can never merit blessing from God. It's the recognition that grace is our only hope. It's giving up on ourselves and finding all we need in Jesus. If you're frustrated at your inability to change, then your first step is to give up—to give up on yourself. Repent of your self-reliance and self-confidence. Your second step is to rejoice in God's grace—his grace to forgive and his grace to transform.

Proud Self-justification

We don't like to think of ourselves as bad people. We don't want to think of our hearts as evil. So we don't take responsibility for our sin. We may admit that we need change, but we don't want to admit that we are the problem. And so we have a number of avoidance strategies. Self-reliance says, "I'll do okay by myself." Self-justification says, "I'm doing okay by myself." Making that claim involves excusing, minimizing, or hiding sin.

Excusing Sin

The first sin began with doubting God's word and desiring created things more than the Creator. As we've seen, these are the characteristics of all subsequent sin. Another feature of that first sin is a common characteristic of subsequent sin: blame, excuses. Adam blamed Eve, and Eve blamed the serpent (Genesis 3:11–13). And today we still try to pass the blame for our sin. We refuse to take responsibility for what we've done.

We blame other people for what they have done. "They provoked me . . . they wound me up . . . they started it . . . I was afraid of what they would say." And we blame other people for what they haven't done. "If you'd helped me more . . . if you'd been there for me . . . if you'd loved me better."

Or we blame our circumstances—our context, upbringing, personal history, or biology (our genes, our chemistry, or the time of the month). Consider what this might sound like for someone who gets angry.

Context: "He just made me so mad. It was so unfair. You'd have done the same if you'd been in my situation."

Upbringing: "I take after my father. He used to get angry. I learned my anger from him."

Personal history: "You'd be an angry person if you'd been through what I've been through."

Biology: "It's just the way I am. I'm hotheaded. There's nothing I can do about it."

There's some truth in all of these explanations. External factors can reinforce or trigger sin. They often shape the form it takes. But none of these factors offers a full explanation for our sin. We choose how we respond to circumstances, and what determines those choices are the thoughts and desires of our hearts. Our sinful hearts portray our actions as inevitable, unavoidable, or appropriate. If someone lets me down, I assume my anger is inevitable, unavoidable, and appropriate. But the truth is that my anger reveals my idolatrous desires. Jerry Bridges says we should use the language of disobedience to describe sin rather than defeat.

> When I say I am defeated by some sin, I am unconsciously slipping out from under my responsibility. I am saying something outside of me has defeated me. But when I say I am disobedient, that places the responsibility for my sin squarely on me. We may, in fact, be defeated, but the reason we are defeated is because we have chosen to disobey.[5]

All our blaming ends up on God's doorstep. We point to other people, our circumstances, or our biology. But what we're saying is that it's God's fault. He allowed these circumstances. He made me the way I am. But James says, "Let no one say when he is tempted, 'I am being tempted by God,' for God cannot be tempted with evil, and he himself tempts no one. But each person is tempted when he is lured and enticed by his own desire" (James 1:13–14). God isn't out to get us. Nor does he put us in impossible situations in which we're bound to sin. It's our own evil desires that entice us. "It's different for me," we say. "My circumstances are unique. Other people have choices, but my behavior's inevitable, so it's not really my fault." We want to be special, even with our sin! But God says, "The temptations in your life are no different from what others experience." Nor is our behavior inevitable: "And God is faithful. He will not allow the temptation to be more than you can stand. When you are tempted, he will show you a way out so that you can endure" (1 Corinthians 10:13, NLT).

Dorothy and Naomi were two elderly women in my church.

Both struggled with physical pain. Dorothy had a problem with her legs. When you met her, she told you about her medical problems in detail. They got her down and made her gloomy. Her conversation had one theme: herself. In contrast, Naomi had had acute arthritis for many years, and her fingers were curled into fists. In the last months of her life, cancer ate away at her body. She was in constant physical pain, often wincing. Yet her eyes always shone brightly, and in conversation she spoke of God's goodness and asked other people how they were doing. The two women faced similar circumstances. If you had asked Dorothy what was getting her down, she would have said it was her ailments. But Naomi responded to her circumstances in a very different way. The joy of the Lord was her strength.

Minimizing Sin

We avoid responsibility for sin by minimizing it. We minimize the offense: "It's not that bad" or "It was only a small thing." We compare ourselves with others: "At least I'm not like him" or "Do you know what she did?" We highlight our goodness: "Overall I'm not too bad" or "I often help others." These are all things people have told me. We call sin a misdemeanor, lapse, slip, or fall. We say, "I was naughty, wild, thoughtless, giddy, defeated, mischievous, clumsy, preoccupied, ill-disciplined." We have white lies, little sins, minor indiscretions. We have a whole vocabulary to avoid naming sin as sin and evil as evil. "It was only a little sin," we say. "Everyone does it." "It's more a personality trait than a sin." But sin is serious—so serious it demands eternal hell or the death of God's eternal Son. True repentance grieves over sin; it never minimizes it.

When did you last tremble at God's Word? "This is the one to whom I will look: he who is humble and contrite in spirit and trembles at my word" (Isaiah 66:2). The humble tremble at God's Word. They don't minimize sin; they tremble before God. But pride makes us deaf to God's Word. We know it already, we suppose, so we don't come to it hungry. We don't engage it as needy sinners. Or else our pride suppresses any conviction it might bring because that would shatter our self-esteem.

"It's not my fault." "It's not a big deal." "Overall I'm a good person." These are ways people avoid taking responsibility for their sin. Our response needs to be, "It *is* your fault. It *is* a big deal. You *are* a bad person."

Increasingly in our culture, self-fulfillment has become the accepted priority. My duty is to myself, people claim, to be the person I want to be or to accept the person I am. So any talk of guilt is seen as an attack on "project me." As a result, even when you highlight my guilt, I'm still the victim. You've just made me feel bad about myself.

I've no desire to make people feel bad about themselves. I want people to know the joy of forgiveness and freedom. But people reject this joy *because* they won't admit they need a Savior. We're not victimizing ourselves when we talk about sin. We're stepping onto the road of forgiveness and freedom. We find forgiveness and freedom from sin when we repent of our sin and turn to God in faith. In fact, there's no forgiveness and no freedom without repentance. And there's no repentance without responsibility. We're not repenting when we pass the blame or minimize our sin. There can be no "buts" in repentance. We can't say, "I repent of my sin, but it's not really my fault." We can't say, "I repent of my sin, but it wasn't really that bad."

I write these words with deep sorrow because I'm thinking of the people I've known who wouldn't take responsibility for their sin. In every case it was a tragedy. Some, I think, were Christians who remained trapped in their sin. Others were unbelievers who will die without God because they won't admit to their sin.

There's an episode of *The Simpsons* in which Homer and Bart drift out to sea in a dinghy.[6] Homer wastes their water washing his socks and eats all their rations. When a rescue plane flies overhead, Homer fires a flare, but it hits the plane. At one point, as they find themselves in thick fog, Homer is in a hysterical panic. "We're doomed; we're doomed," he cries. Then the fog clears, and a boat drifts into view. "Are you okay?" someone calls. But Homer is a typical man who won't admit his need. So he shouts back, "Yup, everything's fine." The fog closes in again, the boat disappears, and Homer returns to his panic.

We can all be like this! We're in desperate straits. We can't rescue ourselves from sin. It fills our lives with tragedy. But when God offers his help, we won't admit our need. We'd rather reject his help than acknowledge our sin.

Hiding Sin

One of the main ways in which pride wrecks the process of change occurs when we hide our sin from others. "Whoever conceals his transgressions will not prosper, but he who confesses and forsakes them will obtain mercy" (Proverbs 28:13). We want our good reputation. So we hide, we pretend, we don't seek help. Such a stance meshes with proud self-reliance. We want to avoid exposure, so we tell ourselves we can manage on our own. But here's what's really happening: we love our reputation more than we hate our sin. We'd like to stop sinning, but not if that costs us people's approval. And that means true repentance isn't taking place. "It is one thing to make a resolution; it is something completely different to repent, diligently seek counsel, and, in concert with others, develop a plan that is concrete and Christ-centered."[7] Think about it: we're prepared to choose sin, reject God, abandon freedom, and even risk hell rather than have people think badly of us.

True repentance lets nothing get in the way of change, not even reputation. Are you confessing your sins to a trusted Christian? Are you going to him or her for accountability? Have you told those individuals, such as your spouse, who are affected by your sin? It's not always appropriate to tell a wide circle of people. But you should freely and willingly confess to those to whom you're accountable. You've not done this yet? You're reluctant? Then your reputation still matters more to you than your holiness. Ongoing guilt makes your opinion the one that matters most; shame makes people's opinions what matter most. Repentance makes God central and accepts his declaration that you're righteous in Christ.

One of the main ways in which pride wrecks the process of change occurs when we hide our sin from others.

Sin is like mold: it grows best in the dark. Expose it to the light, and it starts to dry up. "Everyone who does wicked things hates the light and does not come to the light, lest his works should be exposed. But whoever does what is true comes to the light, so that it may be clearly seen that his works have been carried out in God" (John 3:20–21). We need to bring our sin into the light. When Terry went to see Bob, no one answered the door. But he could see the curtains twitching and hear the sound of footsteps. Bob had got drunk again and had blown his wages. Now he was hiding (badly) for fear of exposure. We can all be like Bob (even if some of us are better at it). His hiding is a picture of the way fear of exposure works. We hide away in the dark. We keep our sin secret. But hiding cuts us off from help. We choose darkness instead of light. Hiding leads to sin, and sin leads to hiding. But grace breaks the cycle. Grace disarms the fear of exposure, bringing us into the light, into the arena of change.

> The gospel, applied to our hearts every day, frees us to be brutally honest with ourselves and with God. The assurance of His total forgiveness of our sins through the blood of Christ means we don't have to play defensive games anymore. We don't have to rationalize and excuse our sins. We can say we told a lie instead of saying we exaggerated a bit. We can admit an unforgiving spirit instead of continuing to blame our parents for our emotional distress. We can call sin exactly what it is, regardless of how ugly and shameful

it may be, because we know that Jesus bore that sin in His body on the cross. With the assurance of total forgiveness through Christ, we have no reason to hide from our sins anymore.[8]

I want to be known for my holiness. But this desire impedes my actually becoming holy. My pride makes holiness my boast, and that cuts me off from my only hope—the grace of God (James 4:6). My pride hides my sin, and that cuts me off from the help of other Christians. My pride minimizes or excuses sin, so I never deal with it with sufficient force. Every day I struggle between the desire to be known as holy and the desire actually to be holy. The truth I need to keep telling myself is that reputation is a small price to pay for the joy of knowing more of God and reflecting his glory. I imagine myself admired by the crowd, and I imagine myself being with God. Being with God seems the far better option. But when I'm among the crowd, the struggle begins again.

Hating the Consequences of Sin but Not the Sin Itself

Often we don't change because we don't really want to. You may react against this. "I have been struggling with sin for years," you may say. "For years I've wanted to be free from it, and now you tell me I don't really want to!"

But the truth is that we often want to change the consequences of sin, but not the sin itself. The desire to change the guilt, the fear, or the damaged relationships can be a strong motive for seeking help. But in our heart of hearts we still desire the sin itself. In moments of temptation we still think it offers more than God.

I often see this in people's lives. People ask me to help them sort out the mess of their lives, but they don't really want to change the behavior that's creating the mess. People want help with debt, but they don't want to change the idolatry of shopping that creates the damaging spending habits. They want help with broken relationships, but they don't want to change the idolatry of self that creates the friction. This is how John Owen puts it:

A man who only opposes the sin in his heart for fear of shame among men or eternal punishment from God would practice the sin if there was no punishment attending it. How does this differ from living in the practice of the sin? Those who belong to Christ, and are obedient to the Word of God, have the death of Christ, the love of God, the detestable nature of sin, the preciousness of communion with God, and a deep-rooted hatred of sin *as sin* to oppose to all the workings of lust in their hearts.[9]

We need to be violent with sin. If we hold back, it's almost certainly because we don't want to be violent toward something we still love.

The answer is always the same: faith and repentance. We need to dig deeper to expose the lies in our hearts and repent of the idols in our hearts. The New Testament language of repentance is very violent. It includes amputating, murdering, starving, and fighting (see Matthew 5:29–30; Colossians 3:5; Romans 13:14; Ephesians 6:13–17; 1 Timothy 6:12). We need to be violent with sin. If we hold back, it's almost certainly because we don't want to be violent toward something we still love. We need to hate sin as sin and desire God for his own sake. Hear John Owen again:

> Look on him whom you have pierced, and let it trouble you. Say to your soul, "What have I done? What love, what mercy, what blood, what grace have I despised and trampled on! Is this how I pay back the Father for his love? Is this how I thank the Son for his blood? Is this how I respond to the Holy Spirit for his grace? Have I defiled the heart that Christ died to wash, and the Holy Spirit has chosen to dwell in? How can I keep myself out of the dust? What can I say to the dear Lord Jesus? How shall I hold up my head with any boldness before him? Do I count fellowship with him of so little value that, for this vile lust's sake, I have hardly left him any room in my heart? How shall I escape if I neglect so great salvation?"

What shall I say to the Lord? His love, mercy, grace, goodness, peace, joy, consolation—I have despised all of them! I have considered them as nothing, that I might harbor lust in my heart. Have I seen God as my Father, that I might provoke him to his face? Was my soul washed that there might be room for new defilements? Shall I seek to disappoint the purpose of the death of Christ? Shall I grieve the Holy Spirit, who sealed me unto the day of redemption?

Allow your conscience to consider these things every day.[10]

A Cross-centered Life

The key to change is continually returning to the cross. A changing life is a cross-centered life. At the cross we see the source of our sanctification (Ephesians 5:25–27; Colossians 1:22; Titus 2:14). We find hope, for we see the power of sin broken and the old nature put to death. We see ourselves united to Christ and bought by his blood. We see the glorious grace of God in Jesus Christ, dying for his enemies, the righteous for the unrighteous. We see our hope, our life, our resources, our joy. At the cross we find the grace, power, and delight in God we need to overcome sin. If we don't come to the cross again and again, we'll feel distant from God, disconnected from his power, and indifferent to his glory—and that is a recipe for sin.

A cross-centered life means an inevitable and resolute rejection of all self-confidence and self-righteousness. The life of Jesus shows us humility, but his cross humbles us. At the cross we see the full extent of our sin: when we get the chance, we kill our Creator. The cross leaves no scope for human boasting. Instead our only "boast" is Christ Jesus, our "righteousness and sanctification [holiness] and redemption" (1 Corinthians 1:30–31). Martyn Lloyd-Jones wrote, "There is only one thing I know of that crushes me to the ground and humiliates me to the dust, and that is to look at the Son of God, and especially contemplate the cross. . . . Nothing else can do it. When I see that I am a sinner . . . that nothing but the Son of God on the cross can save me, I'm humbled to the dust. . . . Nothing but the cross can give us this spirit of humility."[11] The secret of humility, and therefore of change, is never to stray far from the cross. It should be often in our thoughts, on our lips, in our songs, determining our actions, shaping our attitudes, captivating our affections.

When we go to the cross, we see our God dying for us. If you let any other god down, it will beat you up. If you live for people's approval or your career or possessions or control or anything else and you don't make it or you mess up, then you'll be left feeling afraid, downcast, or bitter. But when you let Christ down, he still loves you. He doesn't beat you up; he died for you.

Let his love win your love, and let that love replace all other affections. The secret of change is to renew your love for Christ as you see him crucified in your place.

> Lord, we come to you, a bless'd and broken people,
> Holding nothing in our hands but sin and shame;
> Knowing keenly all the conflicts of a prideful heart
> That loves its fame and hates your name.
>
> So we come to you without a single credit,
> Clinging only to the precious cross of Christ,
> Where the Lion on the throne who is the Lamb of God
> Gave up his life in sacrifice.
>
> Yet we try to live our lives each day without you;
> Try to find ourselves in things that fade away;
> Find importance in the things we do and not in you;
> Like fools at play, we run astray.
>
> So we come to you to glory in your mercy;
> Come to call each other back to your great love;
> Come to leave behind our idols and our substitutes
> And fix our love on God alone.
>
> There is mercy without measure in your death, Lord,
> There is no other place where sinful men may hide,
> And so we run to find the grace that is made ours in you,
> We will live our lives where our great Savior died:
> At the cross, the cross of Christ.[12]

Reflection

John Flavel identified six arguments Satan uses in tempting us, together with model responses.[13] Spot the voice of temptation in your life, and identify how you should respond. You might like to ask two people to read it aloud as a dialogue.

1. *The pleasure of sin*

Temptation: Look at my smiling face, and listen to my charming voice. Here is pleasure to be enjoyed. Who can stay away from such delights?

The believer: The pleasures of sin are real, but so are the pangs of conscience and the flames of hell. The pleasures of sin are real, but pleasing God is much sweeter.

2. *The secrecy of sin*

Temptation: This sin will never disgrace you in public because no one will ever find out.

The believer: Can you find somewhere without the presence of God for me to sin?

3. *The profit of sin*

Temptation: If you just stretch your conscience a little, you'll gain so much. This is your opportunity.

The believer: What do I benefit if I gain the whole world but lose my own soul? I won't risk my soul for all the good in this world.

4. *The smallness of sin*

Temptation: It's only a little thing, a small matter, a trifle. Who else would worry about such a trivial thing?

The believer: Is the majesty of heaven a small matter too? If I commit this sin, I will offend and wrong a great God. Is there any little hell to torment little sinners? Great wrath awaits those the world thinks are little sinners. The less the sin, the less the reason to commit it! Why should I be unfaithful toward God for such a trifle?

5. The grace of God

Temptation: God will pass over this as a weakness. He won't make a big deal of it.

The believer: Where do I find a promise of mercy to presumptuous sinners? How can I abuse such a good God? Shall I take God's glorious mercy and make it a reason to sin? Shall I wrong him because he's good?

6. The example of others

Temptation: Better people than you have sinned in this way. And plenty of people have been restored after committing this sin.

The believer: God didn't record the examples of good people sinning for me to copy, but to warn me. Am I willing to feel what they felt for sin? I dare not follow their example in case God plunges me into the deeps of horror into which he cast them.

Change Project

What stops you from changing?

Whom or what do you blame for your sin?
Think about your change project. Do you ever hear yourself thinking or saying one of the following?

- They provoke me.
- If they'd only help me or love me more.
- I take after my family.
- It's the way I am.
- People don't understand what it's like for me.
- It's my background.
- It's so unfair.
- Anyone would react the way I do.

Whom or what do you blame for your behavior or emotions?

Think about your change project. Is there someone else who feels guilty for your behavior or emotions in this area? This may be because you've found ways of shifting the blame onto them.

How do you minimize your sin?

Think about your change project. Do you ever hear yourself thinking or saying one of the following?

- It's not that bad.
- It's only a small thing.
- What about what others do?
- Overall I'm not too bad.
- Look at the good things I've done.
- Everyone else does it.
- It seemed the best thing to do.

How do you minimize and excuse your behavior or emotions?

How do you avoid taking responsibility?

When you talk about your change project:

- Do you ever say "but"? What comes after the word "but"?
- Do you ever say "if only"? What comes after the words "if only"?

Do you really want to change?

Do you just want to avoid the consequences of your sin or the shame of your sin?

Think about whether any of the following statements are true for you:[14]

- You want change, but without having to break a sweat.
- You want it because you are supposed to want it.
- You want it, but not at the cost of saying no forever.
- You want it—sometimes.
- You want it—tomorrow.
- You want it, but you're waiting for God to remove your cravings first.
- You want it simply because it will make life easier.

Does your repentance have the characteristics described in 2 Corinthians 7:8–13?

- Are you serious about holiness and eager to change?
- Are you angry about your sin and alarmed about where it might lead?

- Do you have a renewed longing for God and a concern for holiness?
- Are you ready to put things right where you have wronged others?

Have you told someone?

- Have you asked someone to hold you accountable in your struggle? If not, then either you fear exposure more than you desire God or you still want to keep open the option to sin.
- Have you said, "I'll tell someone if I ever do it again"? This is a stalling tactic. Get serious about change by telling someone.

Write a summary of the typical ways in which you excuse, minimize, or hide your sins so you can spot them quickly in the future.

CHAPTER EIGHT

WHAT STRATEGIES WILL REINFORCE YOUR FAITH AND REPENTANCE?

By now you may have identified what lies behind your sinful behavior or emotions and the truth you need to turn to in faith. You may have identified the idolatrous desires you need to turn from in repentance. Sadly, however, understanding doesn't equal change. Understanding can be a big step forward. Now we know what we need to do. Even if you haven't fully analyzed your heart—and there may be issues behind issues—you still know the gospel truths and gospel disciplines that will set you free. But the gospel disciplines of faith and repentance are a daily struggle. So the question is: *What strategies do you need to put in place to reinforce your faith and repentance?*

> Do not be deceived: God is not mocked, for whatever one sows, that will he also reap. For the one who sows to his own flesh will from the flesh reap corruption, but the one who sows to the Spirit will from the Spirit reap eternal life. (Galatians 6:7–8)

There is, says Paul, a principle in the world God has made: *a man reaps what he sows*. It's true in agriculture, and it's true in our spiritual lives. Only in fairy stories do you plant beans and reap magic stalks with treasure at the end. Joshua Harris comments:

> What you see in your spiritual life today is the direct result of what you've put in the soil of your life in days past. . . . The difference between the person who grows in holiness and the one who

doesn't is not a matter of personality, upbringing, or gifting; the difference is what each has planted into the soil of his or her heart and soul. So holiness isn't a mysterious spiritual state that only an elite few can reach. It's more than an emotion, or a resolution, or an event. Holiness is a harvest.[1]

What, then, does Paul mean by sowing to the sinful nature and sowing to the Spirit? He has just said, "Walk by the Spirit, and you will not gratify the desires of the flesh. For the desires of the flesh are against the Spirit, and the desires of the Spirit are against the flesh" (Galatians 5:16–17). Our sinful nature has idolatrous desires that cause sinful behavior and emotions. But the Spirit has placed in the heart of every Christian a new desire: the desire for holiness. So we sow to the flesh whenever we do something that strengthens or provokes our sinful desires. We sow to the Spirit whenever we strengthen our Spirit-inspired desire for holiness.

We've seen that we can't change ourselves. It's God who changes us. But we participate in the process through faith and repentance. Faith and repentance are the only true gospel disciplines. It's important to see not sowing to the sinful nature and sowing to the Spirit in this context. They're not rules or disciplines, reentering by the back door. They address our heart and its desires. Not sowing to the sinful nature is all about reinforcing repentance. Sowing to the Spirit is about reinforcing faith.

not sowing to the sinful nature	=	saying no to whatever strengthens my sinful desires	=	reinforcing repentance
sowing to the Spirit	=	saying yes to whatever strengthens my Spirit-inspired desires	=	reinforcing faith

Avoiding Whatever Provokes Sinful Desires

Not sowing to the sinful nature means avoiding situations in which our sinful desires will be provoked. We can't change ourselves simply by avoiding temptation: change must begin within our hearts. But avoiding temptation does have a role to play. It's never the whole solution, but it's part of the solution. As my friend Samuel puts it, "Avoidance buys us time." Sometimes sinful desires feel strong. But if there's no stimulation for those desires, there's time for the truth to prevail in our hearts. We're particularly vulnerable to temptation when we're hungry, angry, lonely, or tired (giving the mnemonic HALT). In these situations we need to take special care. You may need to ensure you have enough sleep or avoid being alone.

The Bible talks about "fleeing" temptation (1 Corinthians 6:18–20; 1 Timothy 6:9–11; 2 Timothy 2:22). We're to run in the opposite direction from anything that might strengthen or provoke our sinful desires. Teenagers commonly ask about dating, "How far can I go?" That's a question many of us ask in other areas. "What's acceptable?" "Is it a sin if I only do this?" And God's answer is, "*Run.*" Don't ask, "How far can I go toward sin?" Ask instead, "How far can I run from sin?"

> No temptation has overtaken you that is not common to man. God is faithful, and he will not let you be tempted beyond your ability, but with the temptation he will also provide the way of escape, that you may be able to endure it. Therefore, my beloved, flee from idolatry. (1 Corinthians 10:13–14)

In every situation God will provide a way to escape temptation. But that doesn't mean we can hang around in tempting situations or flirt with sinful desires. "*Therefore,*" says Paul. God provides a way of escape, and *therefore* we should use it.

I have a friend who struggles with alcoholism. After a couple of pints the alcohol seems to take over. By that point the battle is lost. But he can choose whether or not to go into the pub in the first place. God always gives us a way out before it's too late. We should take that escape route—and then run.

Avoiding Whatever Strengthens Sinful Desires

Most of our sinful desires can be fed by things in our culture. The lies behind our sins are lies perpetuated at a community level. The

Bible calls this influence "the world." Sometimes the Bible uses the term *world* to describe the object of God's love (John 3:16). But it also uses the term to describe human society in opposition to God. The world around us celebrates sinful desires and spreads lies about God. We can't avoid living in a ghetto. But we can and should take steps to reduce its influence on us.

> Do not love the world or the things in the world. If anyone loves the world, the love of the Father is not in him. For all that is in the world—the desires of the flesh and the desires of the eyes and pride in possessions—is not from the Father but is from the world. And the world is passing away along with its desires, but whoever does the will of God abides forever. (1 John 2:15–17)

I have a distinct memory that I've retained for over twenty years. Some Christian friends and I had been talking about the kind of comedy we enjoyed. So I played them a favorite extract. I could immediately sense them wincing at the sexual innuendo. In that moment I realized I'd been exposing myself to corrupting influences. This proved a key moment in my Christian growth. We need to get into the habit of turning off the television or radio. God is not mocked. A man reaps what he sows.

Christians have traditionally spoken of the world, the flesh (i.e., the sinful nature), and the devil as the three threats to a Christian. They all work together. The world is under the control of the evil one, so he spreads his lies through the culture of the world (1 John 5:19). And these lies resonate with, and reinforce, our own sinful desires (1 John 2:16). The question is, which voice(s) are you listening to? The voices of the world, the flesh, and the devil? Or the word of God? As Psalm 1 reminds us, blessing comes when we screen out the voices of the world and listen instead to the Word of God.

> Blessed is the man
> who walks not in the counsel of the wicked,
> nor stands in the way of sinners,
> nor sits in the seat of scoffers;
> but his delight is in the law of the LORD,

and on his law he meditates day and night.
He is like a tree
planted by streams of water,
that yields its fruit in its season,
and its leaf does not wither.
In all that he does, he prospers.
The wicked are not so,
but are like chaff that the wind drives away. (vv. 1–4)

Saying No to Sinful Desires

What, then, does it mean in practice to say no to whatever might provoke or strengthen our sinful desires? Here are some possibilities.

Jack struggled with lust. He realized he had to stop undressing women with his eyes, watching movies with sex scenes, and watching late-night television on his own. When he did see sexual images, he made an effort to think about the goodness of God. He installed anti-porn software on his computer and got a friend to keep him accountable.

Carla struggled with the desire to be loved. She threw out her low-cut tops and short skirts. She decided to stop flirting for fun. She stopped watching romantic films, reading romantic fiction, and daydreaming about romantic relationships.

Colin always wanted to be in control. So at work he stopped monitoring tasks he'd delegated. At first he worried about them, but he refused to let himself check up on people. He put his electronic personal organizer in a drawer and went back to a paper diary. At home he threw away his lists. He decided not to plan his Saturdays but take them as they came.

Emma found refuge in shopping. She cut out window-shopping and browsing online. She went shopping only when she needed something and always used a shopping list. She hit the TV mute button during the commercials, canceled her shopping catalogs, and stopped buying glossy magazines.

Jamal knew he had a tendency to be self-absorbed. He stopped keeping his blog because it encouraged him to think of himself as the center of his world. He stopped having fantasies in which he was the hero and started volunteering in a local shelter for the homeless.

Drinking was an issue for Kate. She felt it best to stop drinking any alcohol at all. She avoided bars and those friends who encouraged her to drink. If she did spend time with those friends, she'd take a Christian with her.

Not all of these actions will apply to you. We all struggle with different sinful desires. Something one person needs to avoid might be safe for someone else. I desire to control the future, which makes me cautious about money; so I decided to stop keeping a record of spending so I'd be more free with money. Someone else might desire meaning and satisfaction through shopping; so keeping a record of spending might be good for them. So these suggestions are not marks of a Christlike life. Paul puts it like this: "'All things are lawful for me,' but not all things are helpful. 'All things are lawful for me,' but I will not be enslaved by anything" (1 Corinthians 6:12).

John Stott sums it up well:

> To 'sow to the flesh' is to pander to it, to cosset, cuddle and stroke it, instead of crucifying it. . . . Every time we allow our mind to harbor a grudge, nurse a grievance, entertain an impure fantasy, or wallow in self-pity, we are sowing to the flesh. Every time we linger in bad company whose insidious influence we know we cannot resist, every time we lie in bed when we ought to be up and praying, every time we read pornographic literature, every time we take a risk which strains our self-control, we are sowing, sowing, sowing to the flesh. Some Christians sow to the flesh every day and wonder why they do not reap holiness.[2]

This can be a hard demand. Indeed, Jesus compares it to amputation (Matthew 5:29–30)! We're likely to feel loss, even grief, when we think about what we must do to starve our sinful desires. They can seem like old friends whom we've loved for many years, and nobody likes killing off their best friends! One man said to me, as we discussed what he needed to do, "I feel like I'll be losing a bit of my heart." I was about to qualify his statement when I realized it's *exactly* like losing a bit of our heart! There's a bit of my heart that is attached to my sinful desires, and I need some heart surgery to remove it. That's why legalism doesn't work.

In a famous sermon entitled "The Expulsive Power of a New Affection," Thomas Chalmers argued that we can't simply tell ourselves to stop sinning. We need to direct the desires that sin falsely satisfies toward that which truly satisfies and liberates—God himself. A renewed affection for God is the only thing that will expel sinful desires.

We're like a child holding a rusty knife. What we grasp endangers us, but we don't want to let go. If you shout at the child long enough, she might reluctantly hand it over. But offer her a lovely new toy and the knife is soon forgotten. Tell someone to stop sinning and at best they may do so reluctantly and partially. But give them a vision of knowing God and his glory, and they'll gladly root out all that gets in the way of their relationship with God (Hebrews 12:1–3).

Sowing to the Spirit

Sowing to the Spirit is about cultivating a new affection for God with its expulsive power. The best way to avoid weeds is to sow other plants in their place. It's the same in the spiritual life. The best way to keep down our sinful desires is to sow to the Spirit. When Paul tells Timothy to flee sinful desire, he always tells him to pursue righteousness in its place. "For the love of money is a root of all kinds of evils. . . . But as for you, O man of God, flee these things. Pursue righteousness, godliness, faith, love, steadfastness, gentleness" (1 Timothy 6:10–11). "Flee youthful passions and pursue righteousness, faith, love, and peace, along with those who call on the Lord from a pure heart" (2 Timothy 2:22).

Sowing to the Spirit means saying yes to whatever strengthens our Spirit-inspired desires. As we've seen, we sin when we believe lies about God. Sowing to the Spirit means filling our hearts with the truth about God. We sin because sinful desires matter more to us than God. We sow to the Spirit when we cultivate our love for God.

Here are seven things that reinforce faith. Sometimes people call them spiritual disciplines. But I believe this is unhelpful terminology. It can make Christian growth seem like an achievement on our part. In reality, it's God who changes us through his grace. The only true spiritual disciplines in the Christian life are faith and repentance, actions that direct our attention to God's gracious activity. So I prefer the traditional term *the means of grace*. These are ways in which God is gracious to us and by which he strengthens his work of grace in our hearts. They are the means God uses to feed our faith in him.[3] This is what sowing to the Spirit looks like in practice.

1. The Bible

The Word of God is perhaps God's primary means of changing us. "Sanctify them in the truth," prays Jesus, adding, "your word is truth" (John 17:17). It's the water by which we're washed, the weapon with which we fight, the tool kit with which we're equipped, and the milk by which we grow (see Ephesians 5:26; 6:17; 2 Timothy 3:16–17; 1 Peter 2:2).

The Bible reveals our hearts. The link between our hearts and behavior is fine in theory, but perhaps when you look at your own heart you see only muddle and confusion. You can't work out the desires that rule your heart or spot the lies that shape your behavior. But "the word of God is living and active, sharper than any two-edged sword, piercing to the division of soul and of spirit, of joints and of marrow, and discerning the thoughts and intentions of the heart. And no creature is hidden from his sight, but all are naked and exposed to the eyes of him to whom we must give account" (Hebrews 4:12–13). "The Bible is like God's great scalpel. It is able to cut through all the layers of who I am and what I'm doing to expose my heart. . . . The Bible by its very nature is heart-revealing. For that reason, Scripture must be our central tool in personal growth and ministry."[4] James describes the Bible as a mirror in which we see ourselves as we really are (James 1:22–25). We should read the Bible not primarily so that we might expound it, but that it might expound us.

The Bible reveals Christ's glory. More important even than revealing our hearts, the Bible reveals Christ's glory. We're changed as we see the glory of God revealed in Christ. We see the light of the glory of Christ in the gospel word (2 Corinthians 4:4–6). In Exodus 33:18 Moses asks to *see* God's glory. God responds by revealing his glory in a *proclamation* of his name: "The LORD, the LORD, a God merciful and gracious, slow to anger, and abounding in steadfast love and faithfulness, keeping steadfast love for thousands, forgiving iniquity and transgression and sin" (Exodus 34:6–7).

The Bible is the source of truth that counters the lies of sin that the world perpetuates. If we are not in the Bible day by day, our hearts will be immersed only in lies.

So the Bible speaks liberating truth to our enslaved hearts, both as we read it for ourselves and as we speak it to one another. The Bible is the source of truth that counters the lies of sin that the world perpetuates. If we are not in the Bible day by day, our hearts will be immersed only in lies. "He that would be holy must steep himself in the Word, must bask in the sunshine which radiates from each page of revelation."[5]

> The law of the LORD is perfect,
> reviving the soul;
> the testimony of the LORD is sure,
> making wise the simple;
> the precepts of the LORD are right,

rejoicing the heart;
the commandment of the LORD is pure,
enlightening the eyes. (Psalm 19:7–8)

You may feel that your soul is sick, confused, or downcast. You may be troubled by worry, sin, problems, suffering, fear, or guilt. In the Word of God you will find medicine for the soul. But prevention is better than cure. The Bible offers the healthy diet of truth that can prevent problems from arising. "I have stored up your word in my heart, that I might not sin against you" (Psalm 119:11). Chris Wright comments, "The more we instill the Bible into our heart, mind, soul and bloodstream, the harder we will find it to sin comfortably. The Bible enlivens our conscience and drives us back to God in repentance and a longing to live as it pleases him."[6] The Bible, by revealing the glory of Christ, reinforces our new Spirit-given desires.

Again and again I've traced a correlation in my life between the neglect of God's Word and spiritual weakness. The Bible is not a magic cure for sin or a talisman against temptation. But the Bible contains the truth about God's greatness and goodness, which undermines the lies of sin. Don't read Scripture each day as a duty to tick off. Savor the truth of God that it reveals. Look for the glory of Christ. Let it interpret your heart. Meditate on what you read. Pray it through. Read it not simply to be informed, but to be transformed and conformed to the likeness of Jesus (Romans 12:2).

2. Prayer

We often complain that we lack time to pray. But everyone has twenty-four hours each day. People who pray more don't have twenty-five-hour days. Our problem is that we decide other things are more important. But when we realize that God is the great change agent in our lives, prayer will inevitably move up the priority list. For some this will require "planned neglect"—deciding to neglect other activities. J. C. Ryle says:

Praying and sinning will never live together in the same heart. Prayer will consume sin, or sin will choke prayer. . . . Diligence in prayer is the secret of eminent holiness. Without controversy there is a vast difference among true Christians. . . . I believe the difference in nineteen cases out of twenty arises from different habits about private prayer. I believe that those who are not eminently holy pray little, and those who are eminently holy pray much.[7]

We should also make prayer our natural recourse in times of temptation. When we see a sexy image, when anger rises in our hearts, when we feel despondent—in all these situations and many more we should shoot a prayer up to God. A child will play happily in her own little world. But as soon as she senses danger, she'll look around for a parent. This is how it should be for the child of God. As soon as we sense danger, we should look up to our heavenly Father for help.

3. Community

One of the reasons God has put us in Christian communities is to help us change. The church is to be a community of change. We'll think more about this in the next chapter, but here are some ways in which the church is a means of grace:

- We remind one another of the truth.
- We are taught the Bible by people whom God has gifted for this purpose.
- We pray together for God's help.
- We model Christian change and holiness for one another.
- We see God at work in the lives of others.
- We remind one another of God's greatness and goodness as we worship him together.
- We are given opportunities for service.
- We provide accountability for one another.

4. Worship

When we worship God, we're reminding ourselves that God is bigger and better than anything sin offers. Worship isn't just an affirmation that God is good. It's an affirmation that God is better. In worship we don't just call on one another to worship God. We also call one another away from the worship of other gods. We remind our hearts of God's goodness, majesty, love, grace, holiness, and power. This isn't just an intellectual recall. God has given us music to touch our emotions. We sing the truth so that it moves, inspires, stirs, encourages, and so transforms us.

When we worship God, we're reminding ourselves that God is bigger and better than anything sin offers.

Have you ever had the tune of a mindless song stuck in your head? You find yourself humming a song you don't even like. The world around us sings a song, and that song often gets stuck in our heads, and we sometimes find ourselves joining in. What the world thinks and desires becomes what we think and desire. To worship God is to retune our hearts.

One special means of grace is Communion or the Lord's Supper. The bread and wine remind us that Christ gave his life to make us holy, to break the power of sin, to give us a new identity, and to make us family. They remind us that we belong to God because we were bought with the price of Christ's blood. The *Book of Common Prayer* summons us to "feed on him in your heart by faith with thanksgiving." The Lord's Supper is a fresh invitation to "taste and see that the LORD is good!" (Psalm 34:8). We discover again the promise of Jesus: "I am the bread of life; whoever comes to me shall not hunger, and whoever believes in me shall never thirst" (John 6:35). We renew communion with Jesus by faith. We're reminded of the truth that the bread and wine represent, and that truth feeds our hearts.

5. Service

We often think of service as the fruit or sign of change. But it's also a means of grace that God uses to change us.

Sin is fundamentally an orientation toward self. Many of us suffer from self-absorption. We're preoccupied with our problems and successes. We bring every conversation around to our favorite subject: me. Or we develop habits of self-centeredness in which we live for our own comfort and security.

Serving God and other people can help redirect us outward, taking our attention away from ourselves. It's a great prescription for people suffering from negative emotions. Paul's advice to a thief is not just to stop stealing, but to do "something useful with his own hands, that he may have something to share with those in need" (Ephesians 4:28, NIV). He wants people to stop thinking about their wants and start thinking about other people's needs.

All sorts of things can happen when we start serving others. We learn from them. We see God at work in their lives. We find joy in serving God. We see prayer being answered. We face situations we can't cope with and discover God's strength. We discover the excitement of seeing God glorified in people's lives.

> If you pour yourself out for the hungry
> and satisfy the desire of the afflicted,
> then shall your light rise in the darkness
> and your gloom be as the noonday.
> And the LORD will guide you continually
> and satisfy your desire in scorched places
> and make your bones strong;
> and you shall be like a watered garden,
> like a spring of water,
> whose waters do not fail. (Isaiah 58:10–11)

What is God's promise to us when we are gloomy, uncertain, dissatisfied, weary, or dry? He will lift the gloom, guide our way, satisfy our desires, strengthen our bones, and water our hearts if we give ourselves in the service of the poor. God made us to love him and love others. We become the people we were meant to be by serving others. When we "pour ourselves out," we find ourselves filled up. If we "satisfy the desire of the afflicted," God will "satisfy our desires in scorched places."

6. Suffering

In the film *The Karate Kid* the young student is assigned a series of tasks by the old master. He thinks they're all meaningless and irrelevant—painting the fence, waxing the car, and so on. But eventually he discovers the repeated hand and arm movements have given him strength, reflexes, and agility—everything he needs to be a great karate fighter! Often the events of our lives appear to be meaningless and irrelevant. But all the time God is training us in grace and godliness.

Suffering stirs the calm waters of latent sinful desires.
It reveals the true state of our hearts.

Even suffering is a means of grace in the hands of God. In Judges 3:1–2 God leaves other nations in the promised land "to teach war" to his people. As each generation confronted hostile armies, it was faced with the need to trust God for itself. Adversity tests, strengthens, and personalizes faith. Sinful desires can lurk in our hearts unnoticed because those desires are neither threatened nor thwarted. But suffering stirs the calm waters of latent sinful desires. It reveals the true state of our hearts. It's God's diagnostic tool, preparing the way for the medicine of gospel truth. Deuteronomy 8:2 says, "You shall remember the whole way that the LORD your God has led you these forty years in the wilderness, that he might humble you, testing you to know what was in your heart." Horatius Bonar comments:

The trial did not create the evil: it merely brought out what was there already, unnoticed and unfelt, like a torpid adder. Then the heart's deep fountains were broken up, and streams of pollution came rushing out, black as Hell. . . . Even so it is with the saints still. God chastens them that He may draw forth the evil that is lying concealed and unsuspected within. . . . When calamity breaks over them like a tempest, then the hidden evils of their heart awakens.[8]

So suffering always presents us with a choice. We can get frustrated, angry, bitter, or despondent as our desire for control, success, love, or health gets threatened. Or we can take hold of God in a new way, finding our joy in him and comfort in his promises.

On May 19, 2006 Nicole Tripp was hit by a car, which crushed her against a wall and seriously injured her. In that moment her life and the life of her parents was turned upside down. Their days were now dominated by the slow routine of her recovery. Her father, author and counselor Paul Tripp, wrote a blog to keep friends informed of her progress. Here's one entry:

It's hard not to look at the day as a day of futile activity accompanied by needless discomfort. You can't honestly look at the day and make sense out of it. . . . Suffering transports you beyond the boundaries of your reason and your control. . . . Suffering is a kidnapper that comes into our lives, blindfolds us, and takes us to where we do not want to be.

But suffering is not just a kidnapper, it is also a teacher. . . . It points you to the fact that there is little that you actually control. It instructs you as to where reliable comfort and sturdy hope can be found. Like a patient teacher with a resistant student, suffering pries open your hands and asks you to let go of your life. Suffering invites you to find security, rest, hope, and comfort in Another, and in so doing, assaults the irrationality of personal sovereignty that is the delusion of every human being. In that way, suffering is not just a kidnapper, and not just a teacher, it is also a liberator. Suffering frees us to experience a deeper comfort and hope than we have ever had before.[9]

7. Hope

John Calvin commends what he calls the "meditation on the future life." We need to dream of the new creation. We need to remind one another of the "eternal . . . glory" that awaits us and that far outweighs our "light momentary affliction" (2 Corinthians 4:17–18; Romans 8:17–18). It means recalling that we're pilgrims in this world, passing through on the way to "a better country" (Hebrews 11:13–16; 1 Peter 1:1; 2:11). "Although believers are now pilgrims on earth," says Calvin, "yet by their confidence they surmount the heavens, so that they cherish their future inheritance in their bosoms with tranquillity."[10] What frees us from the vain pursuit of earthly treasure is the hope of treasure in heaven (Matthew 6:19–20; 1 Timothy 6:17–19).

Meditation on the future life is closely linked with the ascension of Christ. By faith we're united with the ascended and glorified Christ. So we fix our eyes on his heavenly glory. "Since, then, you have been raised with Christ, set your hearts on things above, where Christ is seated at the right hand of God" (Colossians 3:1, NIV). It's with eyes fixed on heavenly things that we "put to death . . . what is earthly in [us]" (Colossians 3:5). Thinking of Christ's return loosens the hold that the world has on us and inspires us to change (2 Peter 3:10–14; 1 John 3:2–3).

Reflection

1. Write your own paraphrase of Psalm 1.

2. Look at the following list of Paul's prayers. For what does Paul pray? How do his requests compare with the sort of things for which you typically pray? Romans 15:5–6, 13; 2 Corinthians 13:14; Ephesians 1:17–19; 3:16–21; Philippians 1:9–11; Colossians 1:9–14; 1 Thessalonians 3:9–13; 2 Thessalonians 1:11–12; 2:16–17; Philemon 4–6.

Change Project

What strategies will reinforce your faith and repentance?

What can you do to avoid provoking sinful desires?

Think about the area you have chosen in your change project.

- In what location are you most likely to struggle or sin?
- At what time?
- With which people?
- Does hunger, anger, loneliness, or tiredness make you more vulnerable to temptation?

What steps can you take to reduce temptation in your life?

What can you do to avoid strengthening sinful desires?
Think about the area you have chosen in your change project.

- Which images, movies, TV programs, books, and magazines strengthen your sinful desires?
- Which people strengthen your sinful desires?
- Which activities strengthen your sinful desires?
- Think about the lies behind your behavior or emotions. When do you see or hear those lies?

What steps can you take to stop your sinful desires from being strengthened?

If you're not sure about an activity or situation, then use these questions based on 1 Corinthians 6:12 and 10:23–24:

- Is this activity beneficial? Does it help me become more like Jesus?
- Is this activity mastering me? Does it strengthen a desire that might control my heart?
- Is this activity good for others? Might it cause another Christian to be tempted?

What can you do to strengthen your faith?
Do you make the most of the means of grace? Identify five practical steps you will start doing or will do differently to strengthen your faith through the means of grace.

Write a summary of the strategies you plan to adopt to reinforce your faith and repentance.

CHAPTER NINE

HOW CAN WE SUPPORT ONE ANOTHER IN CHANGING?

He'd passed up the opportunity a hundred times before. But, taking himself by surprise, he decided to go for it today. He spluttered something about having something to say. Now he was beyond the point of no return. There were four other people around the table at their lunchtime prayer meeting, all looking at him warmly. He took a deep breath and told them, confessing years of sin.

For Stephen, it was the turning point. Three years later that moment is still etched on his mind. But those three years have been years of joy and freedom and growth.

God is in the business of change, and he's placed us in a community of change. The church is one of God's means of grace to reinforce our faith and repentance, but it's also a channel for the other means of grace. I'm holding a book on holiness in my hand that has a picture on the cover of a person walking alone along a beach. The message is that holiness is about me and God. But change in the Bible is never a solo project. Change is a community project.

A Community of Change

Paul talks about the church as a community of change in Ephesians 4. He begins by urging us to "walk in a manner worthy of the calling to which you have been called." Through the death of Jesus we have become a home for God (2:22) and a showcase for his wisdom (3:10). Your local church is that home and that showcase in your area. This means that *change is a community project.*

Change Is a Community Process

Change is a community project because it's a community process as well as an individual process. When Paul talks about becoming mature, he's talking about the body of Christ as a whole (4:12–13). It's the Christian community together that displays God's wisdom. We make God known not just as individuals, but through our life together and our love for one another (John 13:34–35; 17:20–23). That's why Paul urges us to be a united community (Ephesians 4:2–6). Our aim is to "grow up in every way into him who is the head, into Christ" (v. 15).

Imagine one of those children's books that have pictures of different people with the pages divided so you can mix and match different heads, bodies, and legs. You flip over the pages to match up the pictures, enjoying the funny combinations as you go. Paul says the church is a body with Christ as its head. Our job is to change the body so that it matches the head. And we can't be the body of Christ on our own. We can't be mature on our own. Change is a community project.

Sin is always a community concern.
Even our private, secret sins affect the community.

This means sin is always a community concern. My sin impedes the growth of the community as a whole. It stops us from growing together as the body of Christ. It has an impact on all of us. Even our private, secret sins affect the community. No one knew Achan had kept the robe, silver, and gold from the defeat of Jericho, but his sin led to defeat for God's people (Joshua 7). My sin stops me from playing the role God intends for me in the way God intends, and this means that the church doesn't grow and reflect its head as God intends.

Community Is the God-given Context for Change

The Christian community is the best context for change because it's the context God has given. The church is a better place for change than a therapy group, a counselor's office, or a retreat center. We grasp the love of Christ "with all the saints" (Ephesians 3:18). Christ gives gifts to the church so we can grow together (4:7–13).

What does Christian maturity look like? It looks like Jesus (4:13, 15). One of the great things about the Christian community is that it gives us models of Christlike behavior. Of course, no one is perfectly like Jesus, but other Christians help us see what it means to walk with God. It's not just godliness we model for one another, but also growth and grace. We model growth as people see us struggling with sin and turning in faith to God.

Every Sunday in our church we give people the opportunity to talk about what God has been doing in their lives during the past week—answers to prayer, comfort from God's Word, opportunities for evangelism, help in temptation. In so doing, we reinforce our belief in a God who is alive and active among us.

One reason the ascended Christ gives the Spirit to the church is to equip each of us with a special gift—our contribution to the life of the church community (4:7). Everyone's contribution matters. "From him the whole body, joined and held together by every supporting ligament, grows and builds itself up in love, as each part does its work" (4:16, NIV). We all have a part to play in building a home for God. We need one another in order to be a healthy, growing church. This means that everyone else needs you, and you need everyone else. You need to help others change. And you need to let others help you change.

Together we extol Christ to one another, and we each bring distinct harmonies to the song. We comfort one another with the comfort we have received (2 Corinthians 1:3–7). Our different experiences of God's grace become part of the rich counsel that we in the church have for one another. Moreover, in the Christian community there is a collective persistence that's stronger than any individual can manage. When I grow weary of speaking truth to a particular situation, someone else will take up the baton. We're like a choir singing the praises of Jesus. No one can sustain the song continually on his or her own, but together we can.

Paul particularly highlights the role of those who proclaim, explain, and apply God's Word (Ephesians 4:11). That's because the Bible is the source of the truth about God, which counters the lies behind our sin. But notice that these leaders don't do all the work of God in the church. Their role is to equip God's people for works of service (4:11–12). It's all God's people who together build up the body of Christ.[1] We work with one another and for one another, so that together we can be mature and Christlike.

Paul says that Christ "makes the whole body fit together perfectly" (4:16, NLT). Your church is not a collection of random people. Christ has specially selected each one to create a perfect fit. You may have chosen other people for one reason or another. But God placed these people in your life to help you change. As my friend Matt said when we were talking about this passage, "I need to give everyone in our church a new merit in my life."

Paul isn't talking about an idealized church with idealized people. He's writing to a real church with real people. He's talking about your church. You can't say, "That's fine in theory, but my church is never going to be like that." God has given these people to you so they can care for you and so you can care for them. If your church isn't what it should be, then start changing it. Start sharing your struggles, and start "speaking the truth in love" (4:15).

Verse 31 says, "Let all bitterness and wrath and anger and clamor and slander be put away from you, along with all malice." These behaviors all have two things in common. First, they all involve other people. Second, they're all symptoms of thwarted and threatened sinful desires. Often we can't spot sinful desires. But when they're threatened or thwarted by other people, we respond with bitterness, rage, anger, brawling, slander, and malice. One of the great things about living as part of a community is that in community people walk all over your idols. People press your buttons. That's when we respond with bitterness, rage, and so on. And that gives us opportunities to spot our idolatrous desires.

God is using the different people, the contrasting personalities, in your church to change your heart. He's using the difficult people, the annoying people, the sinful people. He's placed you together so you can rub off each other's rough edges. It's as if God has put us, like rocks, into a bag and is shaking us about so that we collide with one another. Sometimes sparks fly, but gradually we become beautiful, smooth gemstones. Remember the next time someone is rubbing you the wrong way that God is smoothing you down! God has given you that person in his love as a gift to make you holy. Sinclair Ferguson comments, "The church is a community in which we receive spiritual help, but also one in which deep-seated problems will come to the surface and will require treatment. . . . We often discover things about our own hearts which we never anticipated."[2]

A Community of Truth

How do we grow more like Christ? We become mature "in the faith and in the knowledge of the Son of God" (4:13, NIV). Immaturity involves being "tossed and blown about by *every wind of new teaching*," susceptible to "lies so clever they sound like the truth" (4:14, NLT). The world, the flesh, and the devil whisper lies that sound plausible. Maturity is being able to say, "No, that's not the truth about God. I'm not going to think or behave that way."

So we grow toward maturity by "speaking the truth in love" (4:15). We build one another up through the words we say. We need to be intentional with our words: "Let no corrupting talk come out of your mouths, but only such as is good for building up, as fits the occasion, that it may give grace to those who hear" (4:29). We need to be communities in which we encourage, challenge, console, rebuke, counsel, exhort, and comfort one another with the truth. We need to be communities in which *everyone* is speaking truth to *everyone*.

In verses 17–24 Paul reminds us why "speaking the truth in love" is central to change. He reminds us, first, in verses 17–19 that the underlying causes of sinful behavior and negative emotions are futile thinking, darkened understanding, ignorant minds, hardened hearts, indulged desires, and continual lust. In other words, we think or believe lies instead of trusting God's Word (see chapter 5 of this book), and we desire or worship idols instead of worshipping God (chapter 6).

> But that is not the way you learned Christ!—assuming that you have heard about him and were taught in him, as the truth is in Jesus, to put off your old self, which belongs to your former manner of life and is corrupt through deceitful desires, and to be renewed in the spirit of your minds, and to put on the new self, created after the likeness of God in true righteousness and holiness. (Ephesians 4:20–24)

What changes us is the truth. "You have heard about him . . . [You] were taught in him . . . as the truth is in Jesus . . . to be renewed in the spirit of your minds." The problem is "deceitful desires" (4:22)—desires that seem to offer more than God, but in fact only enslave us. The answer is "the truth . . . in Jesus." The truth of Jesus sets us free by giving us new desires for God.

So Paul says to the church, "Therefore each of you must put off falsehood and speak truthfully to his neighbor, for we are all members of one body" (4:25, NIV). Paul isn't just saying, "Don't tell fibs." We're to "put off falsehood" just as we put off the "old self" (4:22). We're to stop perpetrating lies that lead to sinful desires. And that's what we often do. People bring their deceitful desires to us, and we stroke them. They say, "My boss made me mad today." And instead of asking whether their anger reflects thwarted or threatened sinful desires, we say, "He sounds terrible. I'd have done the same." People bring their moans to us, and we join in. People tell us what they covet, and we extol its worth with them, in effect saying, "Yes, this is an idol worth worshipping." Instead, the truth we're to speak to one another is "the truth in Jesus." We're to remind one another of the greatness and goodness of God revealed in Jesus.

Where once we were dominated by the desires of the sinful nature, now we are new creations with new desires. Where once we were under Satan's control, now we are led by the Spirit. And where once we heard only the voice of the world, now we have the voice of the Christian community.

"Let us consider how to stir up one another to love and good works," says Hebrews, "not neglecting to meet together, as is the habit of some, but encouraging one another, and all the more as you see the Day drawing near" (Hebrews 10:24–25). We meet together so we can encourage one another. We come together to proclaim the worth of God to one another. We're to address psalms, hymns, and spiritual songs to one another (Ephesians 5:19–20). Whenever we meet, we're to remind one another of the greatness and goodness of God so we will be "making melody to the Lord" with our hearts instead of worshipping idolatrous desires.

This requires so much more than attending church each Sunday. We need to be sharing our lives together. Every day the world, the flesh, and the devil perpetuate deceitful desires. We need a daily dose of truth. "Take care, brothers, lest there be in any of you an evil, unbelieving heart, leading you to fall away from the living God. But exhort one another every day, as long as it is called 'today,' that none of you may be hardened by the deceitfulness of sin" (Hebrews 3:12–13). We're to encourage one another daily. Every day our hearts teeter on the brink of becoming sinful, unbelieving, hardened, and deceived. Every day we need people who will speak truth to us.

Sometimes you hear people say, "You mustn't let other Christians become a crutch you lean on." But that kind of sentiment reflects the individualism of our culture, which values a rugged, self-sufficient spirit. People don't call the Bible a crutch. If we were ever to face solitary confinement, I'm sure God would prove himself sufficient for us. But in the meantime God himself has given us both the Bible and the Christian community to help us persevere and grow. What we do need to watch is becoming dependent on particular individuals. That is usually unhealthy. Christ is our Savior, and we need people to point us to him. We don't want substitute saviors—people who solve our problems or give us reassurance when we should be looking to Christ. God has given us the Christian community not as a substitute for Christ but as a pointer to Christ. The truth we speak to one another is "the truth in Jesus" (Ephesians 4:21).

Paul talks about "speaking the truth in love" (v. 15). Love without truth is like doing heart surgery with a wet fish. But truth without love is like doing heart surgery with a hammer. We will speak the truth effectively only in the context of loving relationships. Moreover, we don't just communicate truth by our words. We should also embody truth in our lives. "No one has ever seen God; if we love one another, God abides in us and his love is perfected in us" (1 John 4:12). We make the invisible God visible to one another in our actions. We're to forgive one another "as God in Christ forgave you" (Ephesians 4:32). We're to love one another "as Christ loved us" (5:2).

Love without truth is like doing heart surgery with a wet fish. But truth without love is like doing heart surgery with a hammer.

I have heard people tell how a Christian was there for them in a moment of loss or crisis—just cooking a meal or holding a hand—and that this helped them see that God was there for them in their darkness.

One way we can speak the truth into people's lives is by narrating how the truth has affected our own lives. This personalizes the truth and helps people see how it applies today. It's also a good way of speaking truth if we lack the confidence or the opening to do so in more direct ways. If, for example, someone is complaining about ill health, we might say, "Yes, sickness can be a real struggle. When I was in the hospital last year I had to keep reminding myself that God is with us in our struggles and that he uses our suffering for our good. I needed to trust God's fatherly care."

A Community of Repentance

The Christian community is a community of confession, accountability, encouragement, and rebuke. These are the ways in which we reinforce repentance for one another:

> If your brother sins against you, go and tell him his fault, between you and him alone. If he listens to you, you have gained your brother. But if he does not listen, take one or two others along with you, that every charge may be established by the evidence of two or three witnesses. If he refuses to listen to them, tell it to the church. And if he refuses to listen even to the church, let him be to you as a Gentile and a tax collector. (Matthew 18:15–17)

> Brothers, if anyone is caught in any transgression, you who are spiritual should restore him in a spirit of gentleness. Keep watch on yourself, lest you too be tempted. Bear one another's burdens, and so fulfill the law of Christ. (Galatians 6:1–2)

We're to rebuke and confront one another (Romans 15:14; Colossians 1:28; 3:16; 1 Thessalonians 5:14; 2 Timothy 4:2; Titus 2:15). It's not the only way we speak truth to one another, but it's an important way. It's also a neglected way. This may reflect a personal reluctance to put ourselves in unpleasant situations as well as a wider cultural disdain for directive interventions. Paul, however, says to the Ephesian elders, "Remember that for three years I did not cease night or day to admonish everyone with tears" (Acts 20:31). He reminds them so they will continue to do the same. Proverbs reminds us that this is often the genuinely loving thing to do:

A lying tongue hates its victims,
and a flattering mouth works ruin. . . .
Better is open rebuke
than hidden love.
Faithful are the wounds of a friend;
profuse are the kisses of an enemy. . . .
Oil and perfume make the heart glad,
and the sweetness of a friend comes from his earnest
    counsel. . . .
Iron sharpens iron,
and one man sharpens another. (Proverbs 26:28; 27:5–6, 9, 17)

Part of our problem is that we don't rebuke one another day by day. So when we do, it creates or exacerbates a sense of crisis. Rebuke becomes confrontation. That may be needed in some situations, but often it can be avoided if rebuke has become a normal part of the way we disciple one another. I need people who regularly ask me about my walk with God, readily challenge my behavior, and know about my temptations. I need my friend Samuel, who often asks, "What's the question you don't want me to ask you?"

Some sins thrive on secrecy. They include sins of escape—things we do when we're feeling under pressure, such as sexual fantasies, pornography, compulsive eating, and addictions. They include sins of the mind—things such as bitterness, envy, jealousy, and complaining. We can become very adept at hiding them, but hiding them feeds them. You feel bad about yourself, so you eat compulsively. You eat compulsively, so you feel bad about yourself. You feel unable to cope with life, so you become a hero in computer games. But your addiction makes the real world seem even harder. The fear of exposure means you withdraw from the Christian community or learn to pretend. But withdrawal and pretense cut you off from the help of the community.

One thing we've learned in our church is that change takes place only when these sins come out into the open. It's difficult, but confession to another Christian will be a big step forward. You don't need to tell everyone, but do tell someone!

What should you do if others confess their sin to you? Speak the truth in love. Don't tell them their sin is understandable or insignificant. That offers no comfort because it's a lie. But we can speak words of comfort because we can speak words of grace. Call them to repent of their sin and to accept by faith the forgiveness that God offers. "You are guilty, but Christ has borne your guilt. You deserve God's judgment, but Christ has borne your judgment." This is true comfort. Embody that forgiveness in your ongoing acceptance and love. But accept people with God's agenda for change. Explore, if you can, the lies and desires that lead to their sinful behavior. Together you may be able to discern the truth they need to turn to and the idolatrous desires they need to turn from. Be proactive about offering accountability. That means asking the right question! Ask them how they're getting on; ask them whether they've sinned again. Be specific—ask when, where, why, how often. Above all, point them to the grace and glory of Christ.

A Community of Grace

The pious fellowship permits no one to be a sinner. So everybody must conceal his sin from himself and from the fellowship. We are not allowed to be sinners. Many Christians are unthinkably horrified when a real sinner is discovered among the righteous. So we remain alone with our sin, living in lies and hypocrisy. But the fact is, we *are* sinners.[3]

We can be communities of repentance only if we're communities of grace. And this means being honest, open, and transparent about our struggles.

We can be communities of repentance only if we're communities of grace. And this means being honest, open, and transparent about our struggles. We see one another as we really are and accept one another just as Christ accepted us.

YOU CAN CHANGE

We must model grace in our welcome of sinners, just as Jesus did. It means I don't pose as a good person. Instead I portray myself as I truly am—a sinner who constantly receives grace from Christ. It means we rejoice to be a messy community of broken people. Here's an entry I wrote in my blog:

> Someone asked me how things were going recently. It's not really a "yes" or "no" ("good" or "bad") question. Life in our congregation is messy. People have a wide variety of problems and many of those problems are out on the table. Are things going well when one of your members has been hauled out of a pub in a drunken state? When people admit problems in their marriage? When people are struggling with depression? Actually I think the answer can be, "Yes, things are going well." A key verse for me in recent years has been the first beatitude, which I paraphrase as: "Blessed are the broken people for theirs is the kingdom of heaven." God's blessing is found among the broken people. I don't rejoice in people's problems, but I do rejoice to be part of a community of broken people. I sometimes describe our church as a group of messy people led by messy people. It's proved a context in which I've been able to address my own struggles.
>
> What's the alternative? One alternative is to be a church in which there's a lot of pretending—where people have problems, but the culture doesn't allow them to be open. Churches like this are very neat and respectable. But I know I'd rather be in a messy church! Mess reflects, I think, a culture of grace. We pretend because either we don't trust God's grace for ourselves or we don't trust others to show us grace.

Here are some responses I received:

> In recent weeks I've been reflecting on how fearful I am of the consequences of people in my church finding out the worst about each other. Will it lead to things falling to pieces? Will it cause pain, conflict, anger, division? Probably, I guess. But why do I fear that? Do I trust that the gospel word is robust and relevant? Do I believe that God will fulfill his promises to a church of broken people? Or does he only deal with sorted, even self-righteous people?
>
> The church has become cloistered communities where people wear masks and very little truth is addressed. . . . I don't want to continue in this way, though it would be easier.

I wonder if I'll ever read an advertisement for a church worker where the church is described as "messy" and "broken" rather than "happy" and "thriving." "Apprentices wanted to work in our needy church with messy relationships and broken people."

Messy church just about sums it up: so many people with so much baggage and chaos all around. I hate respectable church, but this messy church is so hard. I'm constantly amazed how Jesus loves his church.

In John 4, Jesus meets a Samaritan woman at a well at noon. "Mad dogs and Englishmen go out in the midday sun," sang Noel Coward. You gather water in the cool of early morning. But she comes at midday to avoid the rest of the community because of the shame she feels. After she's met Jesus, however, she runs to the community she's been avoiding and says, "Come, see a man who told me all that I ever did" (v. 29). The good news for her was that Jesus told her everything she had ever done and still offered her living water! She no longer had to hide. And it's this testimony that draws the townspeople to Jesus. We can confess our sin to one another because there's no longer any need to hide. Grace sets us free.

Why don't we look to one another for support in change? Why don't we open up to others? Why do we avoid messy relationships? No doubt there are many reasons. We're too busy, too independent, too fearful, too self-absorbed. But if we truly believed that Jesus has given us the Christian community to help us change, then we would make it a priority.

Reflection

Here's a list of things the New Testament says we are to do (or not do) for one another in the church:

- Be at peace with one another, forgiving, agreeing, humble, accepting, forbearing, living in harmony, and greeting one another with a kiss.
- Do not judge, lie, or grumble to one another.
- Show hospitality to one another.

- Confess our sins to one another.
- Be kind, concerned, devoted, serving, and doing good to one another.
- Instruct and teach one another.
- Admonish, exhort, and stir up one another.
- Comfort and encourage one another.[4]

Which of these do you think you as an individual are good at and not so good at?

Which of these do you think you as a church are good at and not so good at?

What stops you from doing more "one anothering"?

Change Project

How can we support one another in changing?

What relationships do you have that help you change?

What opportunities do you have to help others change?

What stops you from having change-oriented relationships?

- "I'm too busy." Are you busy because you feel the need to be in control or on top of things? To prove yourself? To get the most from life? To earn the approval of others?
- "I don't need help." Do you sometimes think, *I can handle this on my own* or *I don't like to trouble others* or *I don't want to be dependent on others*?
- "I'm afraid of what might happen." Do you avoid close relationships because they might get messy or because you fear being vulnerable or exposed?
- "I have enough problems of my own." Do you think mainly about what other Christians can do for you? Are most of your conversations with Christians about you?

Do any of these statements apply to you? What do they reveal about your attitude toward God? What lies do they express? What is the truth you need to turn to?

Is your church a community of grace?

- Are people open about their sin, or is there a culture of pretending?
- Is community life messy or sanitized?
- Are broken people attracted to your community?
- Is conflict out in the open, or is it suppressed?
- Are forgiveness and reconciliation actively pursued?
- Do you constantly return to the cross in your conversation, prayers, and praise?

How can you make your Christian friendships more change-oriented?

Do you have Christian friendships that are not change-oriented? Think about a first move you could make so that you start helping one another change. For example, you could:

- Talk about your own struggle with sin.
- Suggest you read the Bible and pray together.
- Ask them about their relationship with God or their change project.
- Call them when you are struggling with temptation.

Think about practical ways in which you can help, or be helped, to avoid temptation or situations that reinforce sinful desires. You may need help:

- *In particular places.* I have a friend who's a recovering alcoholic. When he wants to watch football in the pub, we make sure someone will go with him.
- *At particular times.* I'm more vulnerable to temptation when my family is away, so I try to arrange to spend time with others.

Write one thing that you're going to do to ensure that you are more supported by other Christians and one thing that you're going to do to provide support for other Christians.

CHAPTER TEN

ARE YOU READY FOR A LIFETIME OF DAILY CHANGE?

There's a lot of talk about freedom of choice today. Whether it's supermarket shelves, health provision, sexual orientation, or even the fate of unborn children, our culture wants freedom of choice. But from a Christian perspective, freedom of choice is in one important sense a myth. Human beings are not free to choose: they're slaves to their sinful desires. We can choose between white and brown bread, whole and skim milk. But we can't choose to live holy lives. We're not free to be the people we should be or even the people we want to be. We're controlled by whatever has captured our hearts, and "those who live according to the sinful nature have their minds set on what that nature desires" (Romans 8:5a, NIV).

Free to Choose, Free to Struggle

But Jesus sets us free. He does this by giving us another desire—the desire to serve and glorify God. We still do what we want, but Jesus gives us a new desire, so now we want to serve God. He does this by putting his Spirit in our hearts: "but those who live according to the Spirit set their minds on the things of the Spirit" (Romans 8:5b).

So now Christians can choose. The old desires still linger. But the Spirit has placed a new desire in our hearts. Each day we're faced with a choice between these two desires—the deceitful desire for sin and the Spirit-inspired desire for God. "Before [a person] was saved there was only one possible outcome in every choice: he was going to sin. But now that he has a new heart, there are two possibilities. He can sin or he can not sin, freely choosing according to his desires."[1]

The Bible describes this struggle between our old sinful desires and our new Spirit-inspired desires as a war. And the battleground is your heart. "Beloved, I urge you as sojourners and exiles to abstain from the passions of the flesh, which wage war against your soul" (1 Peter 2:11). "For the sinful nature desires what is contrary to the Spirit, and the Spirit what is contrary to the sinful nature. They are in conflict with each other, so that you do not do what you want" (Galatians 5:17, NIV). When we want to follow our sinful desires, the Spirit opposes us. When we want to follow our Spirit-inspired desire for holiness, the sinful nature opposes us. We never quite do what we want, for our old sinful nature stops us from serving wholeheartedly and the Spirit stops us from sinning wholeheartedly. No wonder we experience life as a battle! So Paul adds, "Let us not grow weary of doing good, for in due season we will reap, if we do not give up" (Galatians 6:9). The question we each need to ask ourselves is: *Am I ready for a lifetime of daily change?*

A Lifetime of Daily Struggle
CHANGE IS A LIFETIME TASK

Change is a lifetime task, not a one-time event. Sanctification is progressive. It takes a lifetime. It's a marathon, not a sprint. Christians are called to a lifetime of change. The habits and thought processes of sin are not easily unlearned. There are few quick fixes. We'll never be perfect in this life, but we can always and should always be changing.

We'll never be perfect in this life, but we can always and should always be changing.

"We are [God's] workmanship," says Paul in Ephesians 2:10. It is as if, suggests Horatius Bonar, God is sculpting us like statues into the image of his Son. Except, he adds, we are not inanimate marble. That would be a simple task. The remolding of the soul is unspeakably more difficult. The influences at work, internal and external, spiritual and physical, are numerous. Yet over the course of a lifetime, without violating our will and yet without fail, God fashions us into the image of his Son.[2]

Sometimes people are dramatically changed, and one area of struggle disappears almost overnight. But this is rare. And even when it happens, plenty of other areas of struggle remain. Most of us find change a slow battle. Analysis can be quick, but change is slow. We mustn't confuse the two. Understanding the lies and desires behind my sin doesn't mean the problem is solved. Now I simply know where the fight is taking place. I know where to deploy my forces. I know the truth I need to embrace. But the struggle to believe that truth continues.

CHANGE IS A DAILY TASK

Faith and repentance are daily disciplines. Turning from sinful desires in faith today doesn't mean that the problem will be gone tomorrow. I may well find myself having to turn from my sinful desires in faith to God today, tomorrow, and day by day after that. I may realize I crave the approval of certain people so much that they've become idols in my heart. I may determine to fear God more than I fear those people, but it will still be a daily struggle to remember that God is greater. I may realize that my identity is defined by the clothes I wear rather than by my relationship with Christ. So I cut up my credit cards and cancel my catalogs. But tomorrow when I walk past a shop window, the struggle in my heart will flare up again.

> The gospel is so foolish (according to my natural wisdom), so scandalous (according to my conscience), and so incredible (according to my timid heart), that it is a daily battle to believe the full scope of it as I should. There is simply no other way to compete with the forebodings of my conscience, the condemnings of my heart, and the lies of the world and the Devil than to overwhelm such things with daily rehearsings of the gospel.[3]

The battle for holiness is made up of what Horatius Bonar calls "daily littles."[4] It's not given to many of us to make life-and-death choices for our Savior. Not many will be called on to recant or be martyred. For us the battle is made up of thousands of little moments—choices between self and service. We fall, not when we face death, but when we face a traffic jam. It's too easy to imagine ourselves as strong Christians who would stand firm in the face of persecution, while every day we let sinful desires control us. We imagine ourselves winning the great battles when all the time we're losing the "daily littles." But the "daily littles" are the stuff of the battle. Bonar says, "The Christian life is a great thing, one of the greatest things on earth. Made up of daily littles, it is yet in itself not a little thing, but in so far as it is truly lived . . . is noble throughout—a part of that great whole, in which and by which is to be made known to the principalities and powers in heavenly places the manifold wisdom of God (Ephesians 3:10)."[5]

We must always be on a war footing. Imagine a soldier in the thick of battle who decides that today is his day off. He unfolds his deck chair, puts on his sunglasses, gets out his paper, and sits in the sun reading. He wouldn't last long! "Be sober-minded; be watchful. Your adversary the devil prowls around like a roaring lion, seeking someone to devour. Resist him, firm in your faith, knowing that the same kinds of suffering are being experienced by your brotherhood throughout the world" (1 Peter 5:8–9). We need to be in a constant state of alert because our enemy is in a constant state of attack (Ephesians 6:14–17). John Flavel says:

> Keeping the heart is a constant work. Keeping the heart is a work that is never done until life is over. There is no time or condition in the life of a Christian which can allow a let-up of this work. . . . A few minutes' break from the task of watching their hearts cost David and Peter many a sad day and night. It is the most important business of a Christian's life. . . . "My son, give me your heart," is God's request.[6]

There are amazing stories of Japanese soldiers defending remote islands long after the Second World War had ended. People found them in a state of battle readiness because somehow the news of peace had never got through. Christians can suffer the opposite problem. Some Christians don't seem to have received the news of war. They act as if we're in peacetime, but we're at war.

We've seen how we're changed by faith. But this is not passive or inactive faith. The Wesleyan and old Keswick traditions also emphasized the centrality of faith in sanctification, but often in unhelpful ways. The Wesleyan tradition taught people to look for a crisis moment akin to conversion that brings you into a state of "entire sanctification." In the Keswick tradition, faith was understood as reliance on Christ that brought you into the "higher life" in which sin, while not eradicated, was repressed by the Spirit. There was continual deliverance from sin.[7]

Biblical change differs significantly from these two approaches. First, sanctifying faith is a repeated act as, day by day, we affirm our new identity in Christ and find greater delight in God than in sin. Sanctification may involve some crisis experiences in which we, as it were, make leaps forward, but it remains a lifelong process.

Second, sanctifying faith is hard, disciplined work. "*Make every effort* to live in peace with all men and to be holy; without holiness no one will see the Lord" (Hebrews 12:14, NIV). It involves the effort, with the help of the Spirit, of affirming the greatness and goodness of God and his gracious work for us. It's an effort to keep believing when the world, the flesh, and the devil whisper lies that conflict with the truth. Such faith is reinforced by the means of grace, which we should use in a disciplined way. We aren't talking about passive faith that waits on God for a special experience that will release us from struggle. Passive faith and legalistic works are not the only options! The biblical option is the fight of faith[8]—an active battle to exercise faith in reliance upon the Holy Spirit. It's about faith driving a thousand acts of the will, making daily choices to see past the lies of sin. Change is a lifelong, daily struggle.

A Lifetime of Hope

Change is a lifelong, daily struggle. But there's plenty of reason to hope. Paul says, "Let us not grow weary of doing good, for in due season we will reap, if we do not give up" (Galatians 6:9). We will reap a harvest of holiness. Change is certain.

I CAN CHANGE

I can change because "I have been crucified with Christ. It is no longer I who live, but Christ who lives in me" (Galatians 2:20). Christ has broken the hold of sin over my life. It's not inevitable that I sin. The old sinful nature has been replaced by a new nature. God has given me his Spirit with new desires to shape my behavior. Sin no longer defines me. Change is certain because of Christ's work for me and the Spirit's work in me.

> *Change will not be easy. Sin is habit-forming—not just habits of behavior, but also habits of thinking. However, change is possible.*

This means that change is always possible. There's no sin that I need be trapped in. There's no area of life that I cannot change. You may have been committing the same sin over and over again for many years. Change will not be easy. Sin is habit-forming—not just habits of behavior, but also habits of thinking. However, change *is* possible. For just as sin is habit-forming, so is holiness. You may gradually find yourself struggling less with certain sins. Speaking truth to yourself day by day will create habits of thinking. Every time you resist temptation, you weaken the influence of your sinful desires.

Christians need never plateau. Many Christians grew quickly when they were first converted. They were full of enthusiasm and change. Then, after a while, they settled down into a routine. All the public, embarrassing sins have been swept away, but now there's little real growth. If change could be represented as a line on a graph, their line has gone flat. Their behavior has changed, but their hearts go unchallenged. It needn't be this way. Change is always possible.

Other Christians worry that they're not growing when they actually are. Often growth in grace means a growing awareness of our sin.[9] We see the dirt in our hearts all the more as we move toward the light of God. As with a computer game in which you progress up through various levels, so it is with sanctification. Level 1 sins are the obvious, clear sins that others see in us. By level 10 we're becoming aware of subtle and deceitful heart desires.

We need to look both backward and forward. When we look back to what we were, we should feel encouraged by how we've changed. When we look forward to what we will be, we should feel the weight of continuing sin in our hearts. If we get the tension wrong between the "already" and the "not yet" change,[10] we'll either have unrealistic expectations of perfection or give up in defeat.

Maybe you've tried changing with a new determination as you've read this book, but you have still fallen back into sin. Please don't give up. Let me summarize what we've seen about change. Is there something you're missing?

1. Keep returning to the cross to see your sin canceled and to draw near to God in full assurance of welcome.

2. Keep looking to God instead of to sin for satisfaction, focusing on the four liberating truths of God's greatness, glory, goodness, and grace.

3. Cut off, throw off, put off, kill off everything that might strengthen or provoke sinful desires.

4. Bring sin into the light through regular accountability to another Christian.

If you resist doing these four things, and we often resist numbers 3 and 4, it's a sign that you still treasure sin in your heart: sin is still more important to you than God. Turn to God in repentance, reflect on sin's consequences, meditate on the all-surpassing glory of Christ, and beg God to give you a love for him that eclipses your love for sin.

I WILL CHANGE

Paul says that those who sow to the Spirit will "reap eternal life." "We will reap, if we do not give up" (Galatians 6:8–9). Change may take a lifetime on earth, but it only takes a lifetime. The process of change will come to an end. One day we will be transformed and perfected and glorified. Not a day goes by but we feel the burden of our struggle with sin. But it will come to an end.

The Mississippi River twists and turns, sometimes in inexplicable ways. But inexorably and inevitably its water reaches the sea. Sometimes Christians flow away from God, but still we move downstream toward the ocean of his love. God never fails. "I am sure of this, that he who began a good work in you will bring it to completion at the day of Jesus Christ" (Philippians 1:6).

God doesn't perfect us at our death or at Christ's return with a wave of a magic wand. It's the culmination of the process of sanctification in which we're currently engaged. As we saw in chapter 1, change takes place as we see the glory of God in Jesus Christ. At present we see his glory by faith in his Word. "But we know that when he appears we shall be like him, because we shall see him as he is" (1 John 3:2). What perfects us is that full vision of God's glory. When faith gives way to sight, when we see the glorious greatness and goodness of God, all desire for sin will evaporate. When we grasp the full extent of God's grace, all our affections will be his forever. "Everyone who thus hopes in him purifies himself as he is pure" (1 John 3:3).

A Lifetime of Grace

I AM A SINNER

Change is a lifetime of daily struggle that will come to an end. But in the meantime it's a struggle. Often we lose the battle with temptation. Sin may not define our identity anymore, but it's still a feature of our lives.

We can't expect to stop sinning completely in this life. We shouldn't hold out this hope to people or claim it for ourselves. Some people in the history of the church, including the great John Wesley,[11] have believed that we can achieve a state of "sinless perfection" in this life.[12] The universal experience of Christians suggests otherwise. Indeed, Wesley never claimed perfection for himself, perhaps because he knew his own heart too well. The great Victorian preacher Charles Spurgeon is reported to have heard someone declare that he had achieved sinless perfection. Spurgeon said nothing at the time, but at breakfast the next morning he poured a jug of milk over the man to test his claim. It soon proved false![13]

The Bible also refutes sinless perfection in this life: "If we say we have no sin, we deceive ourselves, and the truth is not in us" (1 John 1:8). Such perfectionism has to employ a sub-biblical definition of sin merely as willful acts of transgression. Wesley thought perfected believers could still commit involuntary mistakes or ignorant errors, but not intentional transgressions. But sin is much more than sinful acts. It's the built-in bias against God that has corrupted our thoughts, desires, and will,[14] making us subject to compulsive behavior and causing us to suppress the truth (Romans 1:18–32). Actions that look involuntary or ignorant actually reflect our deep-seated corruption. Finally, assuming perfection is the sort of pride that leads to a fall. If we think we've risen above the daily struggle with sin, then the devil may move in for the kill.

But this creates an apparent discrepancy. Sin is never inevitable because Jesus has broken the power of sin (1 John 3:4–6). Yet it is inevitable that I'll continue to sin in this life (1 John 1:9–2:2). The truth is that I'm not bound to commit any particular sin, but I still make choices to sin because my desires have not yet been completely transformed. "There remains in a regenerate man a smoldering cinder of evil, from which desires continually leap forth to allure and spur him to commit sin."[15] And my desires have not been completely transformed because I've not yet seen God as he truly is. My faith is not strong enough to grasp what one day I'll see—the true greatness and goodness of God. It is only when God appears and we see him as he is that we shall be like him (1 John 3:2).

I AM RIGHTEOUS

"If we say we have no sin, we deceive ourselves, and the truth is not in us," says the apostle John. But he continues, "If we confess our sins, he is faithful and just to forgive us our sins and to cleanse us from all unrighteousness" (1 John 1:8–9). I've written this book so that you might not sin. We can change because of Christ's work for us and the Spirit's work in us. But in this life we'll still sin. I'm still a sinner, and I'll be a sinner until the day I die or Christ returns. But God is also gracious, and he'll be gracious until the day I die and for all eternity. Christ has died for my sins, and his death is effective until the day I die and for all eternity. I'm a sinner, but I'm a justified sinner. The Reformers had a Latin phrase to capture this truth: *semper peccator, semper iustus*: "always a sinner, always justified." I still sin, but in Christ God declares me to be righteous here and now.

*Sin is never the last word for the children of God.
Grace is always the last word.
If we confess our sins to God, he is faithful.
He'll keep his promise to forgive.*

So we needn't and shouldn't despair. If we think of ourselves only as failed sinners, then we may feel disqualified from Christian service and settle for a compromised life. You are a justified saint, equipped for battle, capable of adventurous, risky discipleship on the front line of God's kingdom.

Sin is never the last word for the children of God. Grace is always the last word. If we confess our sins to God, he is faithful. He'll keep his promise to forgive. Jesus said of the Communion wine, "This is my blood of the covenant, which is poured out for many for the forgiveness of sins" (Matthew 26:28). God is faithful to that covenant. And God is just: he will not penalize you when Christ has already borne the penalty of your sin.

> My little children, I am writing these things to you so that you may not sin. But if anyone does sin, we have an advocate with the Father, Jesus Christ the righteous. He is the propitiation for our sins, and not for ours only but also for the sins of the whole world. (1 John 2:1–2)

There is hope for a change. That hope is not in counselors or methods or rules. That hope is a great and gracious Savior who has broken the power of sin and placed his life-giving Spirit in our hearts. He calls us to look beyond the lies of sin to the glory of God. He calls us to believe by faith that God is bigger and better than anything sin offers. He calls us to turn in repentance from the idolatrous desires of our hearts that enslave and corrode to find true and lasting and satisfying joy in God. Our gracious Savior, who died for us "while we were [God's] enemies," invites us to "with confidence draw near to the throne of grace, that we may receive mercy and find grace to help in time of need" (Romans 5:10; Hebrews 4:16).

Reflection

Here's a summary of what we've seen in this chapter:

- Change is a lifetime task.
- Change is a daily task.
- I can change.
- I will change.

- I am a sinner.
- I am righteous.

Think about each of these truths in turn. What happens if you don't believe these truths? How would you behave? Can you see any signs of this behavior in your life?

Change Project

Are you ready for a lifetime of daily change?

Are you hoping for instant change?

Think about your change project.

- Are you expecting a solution that will make the problem or sin go away?
- Have you ever thought you had "solved" it in the past?
- Are you hoping you can stop working on it?
- Are you ready for a daily struggle?

You may need to be more realistic about sin in your heart.

Are you frustrated by your lack of change?

- Do you feel you've reached a plateau in your Christian life?
- Are you discouraged by your lack of change?
- Do you feel you're going backwards?
- In the past, have you focused on behavioral change rather than heart change?
- How have you changed over the past year? Over the past five years?

You may need to have more confidence in God's work in your life.

What do you do when you sin?

- Do you feel God loves you less?
- Do you feel God blesses you less?
- Do you feel you need to make it up to God?
- Do you feel disqualified from Christian service?

None of these statements is true. God's love is constant. He doesn't love us less or bless us less when we sin. After all, Jesus died for us when we were sinners and enemies of God (Romans 5:6–10). We need not and cannot make it up to God. Christ paid the price of our sin in full on the cross.

You may need to have more confidence in God's grace and Christ's finished work.

Write out one truth you need to remember as you face a lifetime of daily change.

Review your change project.

Look back over what you've written at the end of each chapter.

- What have you learned about yourself?
- What have you learned about God?
- What have you learned about change?
- What have you started doing or thinking?
- What do you still need to do or think?

FURTHER READING

Berkouwer, G. C. *Faith and Sanctification*. Grand Rapids: Eerdmans, 1952.

Bridges, Jerry. *The Discipline of Grace*. Colorado Springs: NavPress, 1994.

———. *The Pursuit of Holiness*. Colorado Springs: NavPress, 1978.

Chester, Tim. *The Busy Christian's Guide to Busyness*. Nottingham, UK: Inter-Varsity Press, 2006.

Cleveland, Mike. *The Way of Purity*. Bemidji, MN: Focus Publishing, 2007.

Ferguson, Sinclair. *The Christian Life*. Edinburgh: Banner of Truth, 1989.

Fitzpatrick, Elyse. *Idols of the Heart*. Phillipsburg, NJ: P&R Publishing, 2001.

Flavel, John. *Keeping the Heart*. Fearn, Ross-shire, UK: Christian Heritage, 1999.

Harris, Joshua. *Sex Is Not the Problem (Lust Is)*. Sisters, OR: Multnomah Press, 2005.

Lane, Timothy, and Paul Tripp. *How People Change*. Greensboro, NC: CCEF/Punch Press, 2006.

Mahaney, C. J. *The Cross-Centered Life*. Sisters, OR: Multnomah Press, 2002.

Owen, John. *Overcoming Sin and Temptation*. Wheaton, IL: Crossway, 2006.

Packer, J. I. *A Passion for Holiness*. Wheaton, IL: Crossway, 1992.

Piper, John. *Future Grace*. Nottingham, UK: Inter-Varsity Press, 1995.

———. *When I Don't Desire God*. Wheaton, IL: Crossway, 2004.

Ryle, J. C. *Holiness*. Cambridge, UK: James Clarke, 1956.

Welch, Edward. *When People Are Big and God Is Small*. Phillipsburg, NJ: P&R Publishing, 1997.

NOTES

Chapter 1: What Would You Like to Change?

1. Sinclair Ferguson, *The Holy Spirit* (Nottingham, UK: Inter-Varsity Press, 1996), 139–140.
2. Thomas Watson, *A Body of Divinity*, 1692.

Chapter 2: Why Would You Like to Change?

1. Cited in Tim Keller, "Preaching to the Heart," audio CD, Ockenga Institute, 2006.
2. John Piper, *When I Don't Desire God* (Wheaton, IL: Crossway, 2004), 16.
3. Cited in Keller, "Preaching to the Heart."
4. G. C. Berkouwer, *Faith and Sanctification* (Grand Rapids: Eerdmans, 1952), 33.
5. David Peterson, *Possessed by God: A New Testament Theology of Sanctification and Holiness* (Nottingham, UK: Inter-Varsity/Apollos, 1995).
6. On duty and joy see Piper, *When I Don't Desire God*, 219–22.
7. Christopher J. H. Wright, *Life Through God's Word* (Kingstown, UK: Authentic, 2006), 60.

Chapter 3: How Are You Going to Change?

1. Adapted from John Flavel, *Keeping the Heart* (Fearn, Ross-shire, UK: Christian Heritage, 1999), 9.
2. Richard Lovelace, *Dynamics of Spiritual Life* (Nottingham, UK: Inter-Varsity Press, 1979), 88–91.
3. J. C. Ryle, *Holiness* (Cambridge, UK: James Clarke, 1956), 32, see also 49–50.
4. Bob Kauflin, "The Fear of Man, Hopelessness, and the Gospel," October 16, 2006, http://www.worshipmatters.com/2006/10/16/monday-devotion-2/.
5. Sinclair Ferguson, *The Christian Life: An Introduction* (Edinburgh: Banner of Truth, 1989), 75.
6. William Romaine, *The Life, Walk and Triumph of Faith* (1771; Cambridge, UK: James Clarke, 1970), 280.
7. This verse is often attributed to John Bunyan, but Charles H. Spurgeon ascribes it to John Berridge, a preacher during the Great Awakening, in *The Salt-Cellars* (London: Passmore & Alabaster, 1889), 200.
8. John Owen, *The Holy Spirit*, abridged and simplified by R. J. K. Law (Edinburgh: Banner of Truth, 1998), 48.
9. J. I. Packer, *A Passion for Holiness* (Wheaton, IL: Crossway, 1992), 173.
10. Marcus Honeysett, *Finding Joy* (Nottingham, UK: Inter-Varsity Press, 2005), 65–66.
11. On the relationship between justification and sanctification, see Ryle, *Holiness*, 30–31 and C. J. Mahaney, *The Cross-Centered Life* (Sisters, OR: Multnomah Press, 2002), 32–33.
12. John Calvin, *Institutes of the Christian Religion*, Vol. 2, trans. F. L. Battles, ed. J. T. McNeil (Philadelphia: Westminster/SCM, 1961), 3.16.1.
13. Anthony A. Hoekema, "The Reformed Perspective," in *Five Views on Sanctification*, ed. Stanley N. Gundry (Grand Rapids: Zondervan, 1987), 65.
14. See G. C. Berkouwer, *Faith and Sanctification* (Grand Rapids: Eerdmans, 1952), 32, 78, 93. See also Walter Marshall, *The Gospel Mystery of Sanctification* (1692; Grand Rapids: Reformation Heritage Books, 1999), 28.
15. John Owen, *Works*, ed. W. H. Goold (1674; Edinburgh: T. & T. Clark, 1862), 3:370.

16. Cited in Packer, *A Passion for Holiness*, 121.
17. Tim Keller, "The Centrality of the Gospel," available online, www.redeemer2.com/resources/papers/centrality.pdf.

Chapter 4: When Do You Struggle?

1. Jerry Bridges, *The Pursuit of Holiness* (Colorado Springs: NavPress, 1978), 84–85.
2. Edward T. Welch, *Addictions: A Banquet in the Grave* (Phillipsburg, NJ: P&R Publishing, 2001), 129–30.
3. Elyse Fitzpatrick, *Idols of the Heart* (Phillipsburg, NJ: P&R Publishing, 2001), 163.

Chapter 5: What Truths Do You Need to Turn To?

1. Cited in John Piper, *When I Don't Desire God* (Wheaton, IL: Crossway, 2004), 17.
2. This analogy is from a sermon by Jonathan Edwards called "A Divine and Supernatural Light," *Works*, Vol. 2 (Bell, Arnold & Co., 1840), 12–17.
3. Walter Marshall, *The Gospel Mystery of Sanctification* (1692; Grand Rapids: Reformation Heritage Books, 1999), 48.
4. D. Martyn Lloyd-Jones, *Spiritual Depression* (London: Pickering & Inglis, 1965), 20.
5. Sinclair Ferguson, cited in C. J. Mahaney, *The Cross-Centered Life* (Sisters, OR: Multnomah Press, 2002), 48.
6. C. S. Lewis, *Mere Christianity* (New York: Harper, 2001), 198.
7. For a worked-through example of how these truths apply to our over-busyness, see Tim Chester, *The Busy Christian's Guide to Busyness* (Nottingham, UK: Inter-Varsity Press, 2006).
8. Edward T. Welch, *When People Are Big and God Is Small* (Phillipsburg, NJ: P&R Publishing, 1997).
9. Ibid., 15.
10. C. S. Lewis, *The Problem of Pain* (New York: Macmillan, 1962), 145.
11. Jonathan Edwards, *Charity and Its Fruits* (Cambridge, MA: Yale University Press, 1989), 180–81.
12. G. K. Chesterton, "The Ethics of Elfland," *Orthodoxy* (Cornwall, UK: House of Stratus, 2001), 41.
13. See Calvin Seerveld, *Rainbows for the Fallen World* (Toronto: Tuppence Press, 1980), 53.
14. The Belgic Confession, §24.
15. Martin Luther, *Treatise Concerning Good Works*, 1520, Part XI.
16. William Romaine, *The Life, Walk and Triumph of Faith* (1771; Cambridge, UK: James Clarke, 1970), 280.
17. Richard Lovelace, *Dynamics of Spiritual Life* (Nottingham, UK: Inter-Varsity Press, 1979), 211–12.
18. Joseph Hart, "Come, Ye Sinners, Poor and Wretched."

Chapter 6: What Desires Do You Need to Turn From?

1. John Calvin, *Institutes of the Christian Religion*, Vol. 1, trans. F. L. Battles, ed. J. T. McNeil (Philadelphia: Westminster/SCM, 1961), 1.11.8.
2. Paraphrased from Martin Luther on the first commandment, in *The Larger Catechism*, Part 1.
3. Cited in Os Guinness and John Seel, *No God but God* (Chicago: Moody Press, 1992), 33.
4. Tim Keller, Church of the Redeemer, *Apprenticeship Manual*, Unit 2.4.
5. David Powlison, "Idols of the Heart and 'Vanity Fair,'" *Journal of Biblical Counseling*, 13.2. (Winter 1995), 36.
6. Tim Stafford, "Serious about Lust," *Journal of Biblical Counseling*, 13:3 (Spring 1995), 5.
7. Elyse Fitzpatrick, *Idols of the Heart* (Phillipsburg, NJ: P&R Publishing, 2001), 80–81.

8. This argument is from Jonathan Edwards, "The Freedom of the Will," *Works*, Vol. 1 (Bell, Arnold & Co., 1840), 1.11.

9. Calvin, *Institutes*, 3.3.12.

10. Richard Lovelace, *Dynamics of Spiritual Life* (Nottingham, UK: Inter-Varsity Press, 1979), 90.

11. Martin Luther, *Lectures on Romans*, Library of Christian Classics, Vol. 15 (Philadelphia: Westminster/SCM, 1961), 128.

12. Calvin, *Institutes*, 3.3.9.

13. Sinclair Ferguson, *The Christian Life* (Edinburgh: Banner of Truth, 1989), 162.

14. See Calvin, *Institutes*, 3.10.10.

15. D. Martyn Lloyd-Jones, *Spiritual Depression* (London: Pickering & Inglis, 1965), 17.

16. Andrew Bonar, *Memoir and Remains of R. M. M'Cheyne* (1844; Edinburgh: Banner of Truth, 1966), 279.

17. Paul Toews, "Dirk Willems: A Heart Undivided," *Profiles of Mennonite Faith*, No. 1 (Fall 1997).

18. David Powlison, *Journal of Biblical Counseling*, 25.2. (Spring 2007), 25–26.

19. From Fitzpatrick, *Idols of the Heart*, 163.

Chapter 7: What Stops You from Changing?

1. Edward T. Welch, *Addictions: A Banquet in the Grave* (Phillipsburg, NJ: P&R Publishing, 2001), 170.

2. Jerry Bridges, *The Pursuit of Holiness* (Colorado Springs: NavPress, 1978), 20–21.

3. C. J. Mahaney, *Humility: True Greatness* (Sisters, OR: Multnomah Press, 2005), 80.

4. J. I. Packer, *A Passion for Holiness* (Wheaton, IL: Crossway, 1992), 120.

5. Bridges, *Pursuit of Holiness*, 84.

6. *The Simpsons*, "Boy-Scoutz On the Hood," written by Dan McGrath, directed by Jeffrey Lynch (November 18, 1993).

7. Ed Welch, "Self Control: The Battle Against 'One More,'" *Journal of Biblical Counseling*, 19:2 (Winter 2001), 24–31.

8. Jerry Bridges, *The Discipline of Grace* (Colorado Springs: NavPress, 1994), 22–23.

9. John Owen, *The Mortification of Sin*, abridged and simplified by Richard Rushing (Edinburgh: Banner of Truth, 2004), 59.

10. Ibid., 78–79.

11. Cited in Mahaney, *Humility*, 66.

12. Christopher de la Hoyde, "A Blessed and Broken People," copyright 2007, used by permission; http://www.thecrowdedhouse.org/?q=node/135.

13. Adapted from John Flavel, *A Saint Indeed*, in *Works*, Vol. 5. (Edinburgh: Banner of Truth, 1968), 477–80; also published as *Keeping the Heart* (Fearn, Ross-shire, UK: Christian Heritage, 1999), 116–21.

14. Adapted from Welch, *Addictions: A Banquet in the Grave*, 215–16.

Chapter 8: What Strategies Will Reinforce Your Faith and Repentance?

1. Joshua Harris, *Not Even a Hint* (Sisters, OR: Multnomah Press, 2003), 162–63.

2. John Stott, *The Message of Galatians* (Nottingham, UK: Inter-Varsity Press, 1968), 170.

3. See, for example, J. C. Ryle, *Holiness* (Cambridge, UK: James Clarke, 1956), 21.

4. Timothy Lane and Paul Tripp, *Helping Others Change* (Greensboro, NC: CCEF/Punch Press, 2005), 2.7.

5. Horatius Bonar, *God's Way of Holiness* (Darlington, UK: Evangelical Press, 1864, 1964), 118–19.

6. Christopher J. H. Wright, *Life Through God's Word: Psalm 119* (Kingstown, UK: Authentic, 2006), 65.

7. J. C. Ryle, *Practical Religion* (1878; Edinburgh: Banner of Truth, 1998), 71, 74–75.

Notes

8. Horatius Bonar, *The Night of Weeping in the Life and Work of Horatius Bonar* (Toronto: LUX Publications, 2004), 36–37.
9. Paul David Tripp, "Control?," June 11, 2006, http://nicolenews.blogspot.com/2006_06_11_archive.html.
10. John Calvin, *The Epistles of Paul the Apostle to the Romans and to the Thessalonians*, trans. R. Mackenzie, ed. D. W. Torrance and T. F. Torrance (Edinburgh: St Andrew Press, 1961), on Romans 5:2.

Chapter 9: How Can We Support One Another in Changing?

1. For a more a detailed discussion of the exegetical controversies in these verses, see Peter T. O'Brien, *The Letter to the Ephesians* (Grand Rapids: Eerdmans and Nottingham, UK: Apollos, 1999), 297–305.
2. Sinclair Ferguson, *Grow in Grace* (Edinburgh: Banner of Truth, 1989), 77.
3. Dietrich Bonhoeffer, *Life Together* (London: SCM, 1954), 86.
4. Mark 9:50; John 13:34–35; Romans 12:10, 16; 14:13; 15:5, 7, 14; 16:16; 1 Corinthians 12:15; 2 Corinthians 13:11–12; Galatians 5:13; Ephesians 4:2, 32; 5:19, 21; Colossians 3:9, 13, 16; 1 Thessalonians 4:18; 5:11, 15; Hebrews 3:13; 10:24–25; James 5:9, 16; 1 Peter 4:8–10; 5:5, 14.

Chapter 10: Are You Ready for a Lifetime of Daily Change?

1. Elyse Fitzpatrick, *Idols of the Heart* (Phillipsburg, NJ: P&R Publishing, 2001), 147.
2. See Horatius Bonar, *God's Way of Holiness* (1864; Darlington, UK: Evangelical Press, 1979), 5–6.
3. Milton Vincent, *A Gospel Primer for Christians* (Bemidji, MN: Focus Publishing, 2008), 14, citing 1 Corinthians 1:21, 23; 1 John 3:19–20; 2 Corinthians 4:4.
4. Bonar, *God's Way of Holiness*, 127.
5. Ibid.
6. Adapted from John Flavel, *Keeping the Heart* (Fearn, Ross-shire, UK: Christian Heritage, 1999), 20.
7. See David Bebbington, *Holiness in Nineteenth-Century England* (Carlisle, UK: Paternoster Press, 2000).
8. See J. C. Ryle, *Holiness* (Cambridge, UK: James Clarke, 1956), 57–60.
9. See J. I. Packer, *A Passion for Holiness* (Wheaton, IL: Crossway, 1992), 156, 221.
10. See Sinclair Ferguson, *The Holy Spirit* (Nottingham, UK: Inter-Varsity Press, 1996), 149.
11. John Wesley, "Sermon on Christian Perfection," *Forty-Four Sermons* (1787–1788; Peterborough, UK: Epworth, 1944), 457–80.
12. See Donald Alexander, ed., *Christian Spirituality: Five Views of Sanctification* (Nottingham, UK: Inter-Varsity Press, 1988).
13. There are various versions of this story. See R. Paul Stevens and Michael Green, *Living the Story* (Grand Rapids: Eerdmans, 2003), 141; and Charles H. Spurgeon, *The Early Years* (1897; Edinburgh: Banner of Truth, 1962), 228–30.
14. See John Calvin, *Institutes of the Christian Religion*, trans. F. L. Battles, ed. J. T. McNeil, Vol. 1 (Philadelphia: Westminster/SCM, 1961) 3.3.10.
15. Ibid.

SCRIPTURE INDEX